CONVERSATIONAL ARABIC QUICK AND EASY

(Lebanese Dialect)

Part - 2

YATIR NITZANY

Foreword

For many years I struggled to learn Spanish, and I still knew no more than about twenty words. Consequently, I was extremely frustrated. One day I stumbled upon this method as I was playing around with word combinations. Suddenly, I came to the realization that every language has a certain core group of words that are most commonly used and, simply by learning them, one could gain the ability to engage in quick and easy conversational Spanish.

I discovered which words those were, and I narrowed them down to three hundred and fifty that, once memorized, one could connect and create one's own sentences. The variations were and are *infinite*! By using this incredibly simple technique, I could converse at a proficient level and speak Spanish. Within a week, I astonished my Spanish-speaking friends with my newfound ability. The next semester I registered at my university for a Spanish language course, and I applied the same principles I had learned in that class (grammar, additional vocabulary, future and past tense, etc.) to those three hundred and fifty words I already had memorized, and immediately I felt as if I had grown wings and learned how to fly.

At the end of the semester, we took a class trip to San José, Costa Rica. I was like a fish in water, while the rest of my classmates were floundering and still struggling to converse. Throughout the following months, I again applied the same principle to other languages—French, Portuguese, Italian, and Arabic, all of which I now speak proficiently, thanks to this very simple technique.

This method is by far the fastest way to master quick and easy conversational language skills. There is no other technique that compares to my concept. It is effective, it worked for me, and it will work for you. Just be consistent with my program. By learning these mere 350 words, which I will teach you in this book, you too will also succeed the way I and many, many others have. This book is *not* a grammar book, nor a phrasebook, it's purely meant to assist in aiding you to communicate in a foreign language.

Contents

Introduction to the Program 6
Travel 8
Transportation 14
City 18
Entertainment 24
Foods 30
Vegetables 36
Fruits 40
Shopping 44
Family 50
Human Body 54
Health 58
Emergencies and Natural Disasters 64
Home 68

Introduction to the Program

In the first book, you were taught the three hundred and fifty most useful words in the Lebanese dialect of the Arabic language, which, once memorized, could be combined in order for you to create your own sentences. Now, with the knowledge you have gained, you can use those words in Conversational Arabic Quick and Easy Part 2 and Part 3, in order to supplement the three hundred and fifty words that you've already memorized. This combination of words and sentences will help you master the language to even greater proficiency and quicker than with other courses.

The books that comprise Parts 2 and 3 have progressed from just vocabulary and are now split into various categories that are useful in our everyday lives. These categories range from travel to food to school and work, and other similarly broad subjects. In contrast to various other methods, the topics that are covered also contain parts of vocabulary that are not often broached, such as the military, politics, and religion. With these more unusual topics for learning conversational languages, the student can learn quicker and easier. This method is flawless and it has proven itself time and time again.

If you decide to travel to Lebanon, then this book will help you speak this dialect.

This method has worked for me and thousands of others. It surpasses any other language-learning method system currently on the market today.

This book, Part 2, specifically deals with practical aspects concerning travel, camping, transportation, city living, entertainment such as films, food including vegetables and fruit, shopping, family including grandparents, in-laws, and stepchildren, human anatomy, health, emergencies, and natural disasters, and home situations.

The sentences within each category can help you get by in other countries.

In relation to travel, for example, you are given sentences about food, airport necessities such as immigration, and passports. Helpful phrases include, "Where is the immigration and passport control inside the airport?" and "I want to order a bowl of cereal and toast with jelly." For flights there are informative combinations such as, "There is a long line of passengers in the terminal because of the delay on the runway." When arriving in another country options for what to say include, "We want to hire a driver for the tour. However, we want to pay with a credit card instead of cash" and, "On which street is the car-rental agency?"

When discussing entertainment in another country and in a new language, you are provided with sentences and vocabulary that will help you interact with others. You can discuss art galleries and watching foreign films. For example, you may need to say to friends, "I need subtitles if I watch a foreign film" and, 'The mystery-suspense genre films are usually good movies'. You can talk about your own filming experience in front of the camera.

The selection of topics in this book is much wider than in ordinary courses. By including social issues as well, it will help you to engage with more people who speak the language you are learning.

Part 3 will deal with vocabulary and sentences relevant to indoor matters such as school and the office, but also a variety of professions and sports.

DISCLAIMER - The use of numerical symbols to identify Arabic accents, in English transliteration, is known as the Franco-Arabic technique. In which three "3" is used to signify aayin عين. Seven "7" is used to signify ha ح. Two "2" is to signify قاف a soft "aه". Five "5" to signify kha خا.

Travel – El Safar السفر

Flight - El Tayaran الطيران
Airplane - El Tiyara الطيارة
Airport – El Matar المطار
Terminal – M7attit El Tayaran محطة الطيران
Passport – Jawez El Safar جواز السفر
Customs – El Gamerik الجمارك
Take off (airplane) – El Te2li3a الطلعة
Take off (airplane) – Betghedir بتغادر
Landing - El Houbout الهبوط
Departure - El Mou8edara المغادرة
Arrival – El Wousoul الوصول
Gate - El-Bouwebe البوابة

This is a very expensive flight.
Hayde re7le ktir (very) ghalye (expensive).
هيدي رحلة كتير غالية.

The airplane takes off in the morning and lands at night.
El tiyara betghedir (leaves) el sobo7 (morning) w btohbot bel lel (night).
الطيارة بتغادر الصبح و بتهبط بالليل.

We need to go to the departure gate instead of the arrival gate.
Lezim nrou7 3ala bouwebit el moughedara badel (instead) bouwebit el wousoul.
لازم نروح على بوابة المغادرة بدل بوابة الوصول.

The flight takes off at 3pm, but the boarding commences at 2:20pm.
Bet2alli3 el tiyara el se3a 3 ba3d el dohr, bass betballich el tal3a 3al tiyara 3al tinteen w 3ishreen da2i2a ba3d el dohr.
بتقلع الطيارة على الساعة تلات بعد الضهر بس بتبلش الطلعة عالطيارة عالتنتين وعشرين دقيقة بعد الضهر.

Where is the passport control inside the airport?
Wen markaz moure2abit jawezet el safar bi-alb (in the heart of) el matar?
وين مركز مراقبة جوازات السفر بقلب المطار؟

Luggage - Chenat El Safar شنط السفر
Suitcase - Chantit El Safar شنطة السفر
Baggage claim - Istilem Chenat El Safar استلام شنط السفر
Passenger – (Male) El Rekib الراكب
Passenger – (Female) El Rekbe الراكبة
Final Destination – El Wejha El Nihe2ye الوجهة النهائية
Boarding - El Tal3a 3al Tiyara الطلعة عالطيارة
Runway - El Madraj المدرج
Line - El Zi7 الزيح
Delay - Te2khir التأخير
Wing - El Jne7 الجناح

My suitcase is at the baggage claim.
Chanti bi-ma7al (is at the place of) istilem chenat el safar.
شنطتي بمحل استلام شنط السفر.

There is a long line of passengers in the terminal because of the delay on the runway.
Fi ktir rekkeb natrin (waiting) bel m7atta men wara el te2khir yali sar 3al madraj.
في كتير ركاب ناطرين بالمحطة من ورا التأخير يلي صار عالمدرج.

What is your final destination?
Shou hyeh wejehtak el nihe2ye?
شو هي وجهتك النهائية؟

I don't like to sit above the wing of the airplane.
Ma b7ebb e23od (to sit) fo2 jeni7 el tiyara.
ما بحب أقعد فوق جناح الطيارة.

Do I need to check in my luggage?
Lezim (must) sajjil chenat el safar?
لازم سجّل شنطة السفر؟

I am almost finished at customs.
Ta2riban (almost) rah khallis bel gamerik.
تقريباً رح خلص بالجمارك.

I like to travel.
B7ebb sefir.
بحب السفر.

International flight – Ra7le Douwaliye رحله دولية
Domestic flight – Ra7le Dekhiliye رحلة داخلية
First class – Daraje Awle درجة أولى
Business class – Darajet Rijel El A3mel درجة رجال الاعمال
Economy class – Daraje Siya7iye درجة سياحية
Round trip – Raw7a Raj3a روحة رجعة
One-way flight – Bas Raw7a بس روحة
Return flight – Ra7let Al 3awde رحلة العودة
Direct flight – Ra7le Moubashara رحلة مباشرة
Flight attendant – Mudifet Tayaran مضيفة طيران

The flight attendant told me to go to the check in counter.
Mudifet el tayaran 2aletli (told me) ta rou7 3a maktab el tesjil.
.مضيفة الطيران قالتلي روح عمكتب التسجيل

For international flights, you must be at the airport three hours before the flight.
Bel ra7le el douwaliye, lezim tkoun bl matar tlet se3at abel (before) el ra7le.
.بالرحلة الدولية لازم تكون بالمطار تلات ساعات قبل الرحلة

For a domestic flight, I need to arrive at the airport at least two hours before the flight.
Bel ra7le el dekhliye, lezim ousal (to arrive) 3al matar 3al alile (at least) se3ten abel el ra7le.
.بالرحلة الداخلية لازم أوصل عالمطار عالقليلة ساعتين قبل الرحلة

Business class is usually cheaper than first class.
Darajit rijel el a3mel 3adatan (usually) arkhas (cheaper) men el daraje el awle.
.درجة رجال الأعمال عادةً أرخص من الدرجة الأولى

The one-way ticket is cheaper than the round-trip ticket.
Ticket el raw7a arkhas men ticket raw7a-raj3a.
.تكت الروحة أرخص من تكت روحة رجعة

Layover / connection – Tawa2of توقف
Reservation – 7ajez حجز
Security check – Fa7es Amene فحص أمني
Checked bags – El Chenat Yeli Tsallamit الشنط يلي تسلمت
Carry-on bag – Chantet 2id شنطة إيد
Business trip – Ra7let 3amal رحلة عمل
Check in counter – Maktab El Tesjil مكتب التسجيل
Travel agency – Maktab Safriyet مكتب سفريات
Temporary visa – Ta2shira Mwa2ate تأشيرة مؤقتة
Country – Balad بلد

I purchased my plane tickets at the travel agency.
Chtrit tiketet el tayaran men maktab safriyet.
شريت تكت الطياران من مكتب السفريات.

I prefer a direct flight without a layover.
Bfadel ra7le moubashara bala (without) tawa2of.
بفضل رحلة مباشرة بلا توقف.

I must make reservations for my return flight.
Lezim e7joz la ra7lte al 3awde.
لازم أحجز لرحلة العودة.

Why do I need to remove my shoes at the security check?
Leh badi echla7 (remove) el sbat (shoes) bl fa7s el amene.
ليه بدي أشلح السباط بالفحص الأمني؟

I have three checked bags and one carry-on.
3andi tlet chenat tsallamit w chantit 2id.
عندي تلات شنط تسلمت وشنطة الإيد.

I have to ask my travel agent if this country requires an entry visa.
Lezim es2alo la wakil el safariyet taba3i iza hal balad byettalab (requires) ta2shiret doukhoul.
لازم إسئله لوكيل السفريات تبعي إزا هالبلد بطلب تأشيرة دخول.

Trip – Ra7le رحلة
Tourist – Seyi7 سائح
Tourism – Siye7a سياحة
Holiday – A3yed أعياد
Vacations – Foras فرص
Currency exchange – Serraf صراف
Port of entry – Bouwebet El Doukhoul بوابة الدخول
Car rental agency – Maktab Te2jir Siyarat مكتب تأجير السيارات
Identification – Hawiye هوية
GPS – GPS جي بي إس
Road – Tari2 طريق
Map – Kharita خريطة

I had an amazing trip.
Kanet ra7le ktir 7elwe.
.كانت رحلة كتير حلوة

The currency exchange counter is past the port of entry.
El sarraf men-ba3d (is past/following) bouwebet el doukhoul.
.الصراف من بعد بوابة الدخول

There is a lot of tourism during the holidays and vacations.
Fi ktir siye7a bl foras wel a3yed.
.في كتير سياحة بالفرص والأعياد

Where is the car-rental agency?
Wen maktab te2jir el siyarat?
وين مكتب تأجير السيارات؟

You need to show your identification whenever checking in at a hotel.
Lezim tfarji (to show) hawitak lamma (whenever) badak tenzal bi hotel.
.لازم تفرجي هويتك لما بدك تنزل بالأوتيل

It's more convenient to use the GPS on the roads instead of a map.
Ahwanlak testa3mil (to use) el GPS badel el kharita 3al tari2.
.أهونلك تستعمل الجي بي إس بدل الخريطة عالطريق

Information center – Markaz Ma3loumet مركز معلومات
Bank - Bank بنك
Hotel – Hotel أوتيل
Motel - Hotel أوتيل
Hostel - Hotel أوتيل
Leisure – Wa2t Faragh وقت فراغ
Driver – (Male) El Seyi2 السايق
Driver – (Female) El Sey2a السايقة
Tour – Ra7le رحلة
Credit – Credit كريدت
Cash – Na2de نقدي
A travel guide – Dalil Siye7e دليل سياحي
Ski resort – Mountaja3 Lal tazaluj منتجع للتزلج

Why is the information center closed today?
Leh markaz el ma3loumet msakkar (closed) lyom?
ليه مركز المعلومات مسكر اليوم؟

When I am in a new country, I go to the bank before I go to the hotel.
Bas koun bi balad jdid, brou7 3al bank abel ma rou7 3al hotel.
بس كون ببلد جديد بروح عالبنك قبل ما روح على الأوتيل.

I need to book my leisure vacation at the ski resort today.
Lyom badi e7joz la-ijazti bi montaja3 el tazaluj.
اليوم بدي أحجز لإجازتي بمنتجع التزلج.

We want to hire a driver for the tour.
Badna nwazef (to hire) seyi2 lal ra7le.
بدنا نوظف سايق للرحلة.

We want to pay with a credit card instead of cash.
Badna nedfa3 (to pay) bl (in) credit card badel na2de.
بدنا ندفع بالكريدت كارد بدل النقدي.

Does the tour include an English-speaking guide?
Domen (include) el ra7le fih dalil siye7e bye7ke 2englizi?
دومين الرحلة فيه دليل سياحي بحكي إنجليزي؟

Transportation – Na2liyet نقليات

Car - Siyara سيارة
Station – M7atta محطة
Train - Qitar قطار
Train station – M7attet Qitar محطة قطار
Train tracks – Sekkit 7adid سكة حديد
Train cart – 3arabiyet El Qitar عربية القطار
Subway – Métro مترو
Ticket – Tazkarah تذكرة
Taxi – Taxi تاكسي

Where is the public transportation?
Wen el na2l el 3am?
وين النقل العام؟

Where can I buy a bus ticket?
Wen fiyi eshtri ticket lal bas?
وين فيي أشتري تكت الباص؟

Please call a taxi.
Please tloble (to order) taxi.
بليز اطلبلي تكسي.

In some areas, you don't need a car because you can rely on the subway.
Bi ba3d el manate2 (areas), ma (don't) bte3tez siyara fik testa3mil el metro.
ببعض المناطق ما بتعتاز سيارة، فيك تستعمل المترو.

Where is the train station?
Wen m7attet el qitar?
وين محطة القطار؟

The train cart is still stuck on the tracks.
3arabiyet el qitar ba3da (still) m3al2a 3al sekke.
عرباية القطار بعدا معلقة عالسكة.

Motorcycle - Moto موتو
Scooter – Scooter سكوتر
Helicopter – Helicopter هلوكبتر
School bus – Bas El Madrase باص مدرسة
Limousine – Limousine ليموزين
Driver license – Daftar Swe2a دفتر سواقة
Vehicle registration – Tesjil Siyara تسجيل سيارة
Vehicle registration – Daftar el siyara دفتر سيارة
License plate – Nomrit El Siyara نمرة سيارة
Ticket (penalty) – Mukhalafeh مخالفة
Ticket (penalty) – Zabet ضبط

The motorcycles make loud noises.
El motoyet bya3mlo (they make) sot (noise) 3ale (high/loud).
المتويت بيعملوا صوت عالي.

Where can I rent a scooter?
Wen fiyi esta2jir scooter?
وين فيي استأجر سكوتر؟

I want to schedule a helicopter tour.
Badi nazzem (to schedule) ra7le bl helicopter.
بدي نظّم رحلة بالهلوكبتر.

I want to go to the party in a limousine.
Badi rou7 3al 7afle bl limousine.
بدي روح عالحفلة بالموزين.

Don't forget to bring your driver's license and registration.
Ma tensa (forget) tjib ma3ak daftar el swe2a w daftar el siyara.
ما تنسى تجيب معك دفتر السواقة ودفتر السيارة.

The cop gave me a ticket because my license plate is expired.
El chorti 3emelli zabet la2enno nomriti khalis-wa2ta (expired).
الشرطي عاملي ضبط لأنه نمرتي خلص وقتها.

Truck – Kamyon كاميون
Pickup truck – Pickup بك أب
Bicycle – Bisiklet بسكليت
Van – Van فان
Gas station – Trombet Benzin طرمبة بنزين
Gasoline – Benzin بنزين
Tire – Douleb دولاب
Oil change – Ghyar Zeit غيار زيت
Tire change – Ghyar Douleb غيار دولاب
Mechanic – Mécanici ميكانيكي

I can put my bicycle in my truck.
Fiyi (I can) 7ot (put) bisikleti bl pickup taba3i (my/mine).
.فيي أحط بسكليتي بالبكب تبعي

Where is the gas station?
Wen trombet el benzin?
وين طرنبة البنزين؟

I need gasoline and also to put air in my tires.
Badi benzin w badi enfokh (inflate) douwelibi.
.بدي بنزين وبدي أنفخ دولابي

I need to take my car to the mechanic for a tire and oil change.
Badi ekhod siyarti la 3and el mecanici la ghayyir el dwelib wel zeit.
.بدي آخد سيارتي لعند الميكانيكي لغير دولاب وزيت

I can put my canoe in the van.
Fiyi 7ot el canoe taba3i bl van.
.فيي حط الكانوي تبعي بالفان

Canoe – Canoë كانوي
Ship - Bekhra باخرة
Boat – Chakhtoura شختورة
Yacht – Yakht يخت
Sailboat - Chakhtoura Chira3iye شختورة شراعية
Motorboat – Chakhtoura Ma3 Motor شختورة مع متور
Marina - Marina مارينا
A dock - El Rsif الرصيف
Cruise - Cruise كروز
Cruise ship – Safinet El Cruise سفينة الكروز
Ferry – 3ebbara عبّارة
Submarine – Ghouwasa غواصة

Can I bring my yacht to the boat show at the marina?
Fiyi jib el yacht taba3i 3ala 3ard (exhibition) el ykhoute bl marina?
فيي جيب اليخت تبعي على عرض اليخوت بالمرينا؟

I prefer a motorboat instead of a sailboat.
Bfaddel chakhtoura ma3 motor badel chakhtoura chira3iye.
بفضّل شختورة مع متور بدل شختورة شراعية.

I want to leave my boat at the dock on the island.
Baddi khalli chakhtourti 3ala el rsif taba3 el jazire.
بدي أخلي شختورتي على الرصيف تبع الجزيرة.

This spot is a popular stopping point for the cruise ship.
Hai el-no2ta (spot/point) hiye no2ta cha3biye (popular) biwa2fo fiya sofon el cruise.
هاي النقطة هي نقطة شعبية بوقفوا فيا سفن الكروز.

This was an incredible cruise.
Kenit hayde el cruise 7elwe (beautiful).
كانت هايدي كروز حلوة.

Do you have the schedule for the ferry?
3andak el-bernemij (schedule) taba3 el 3ebbara?
عندك البرنامج تبع العبّارة؟

The submarine is yellow.
El ghouwasa lawna (color) asfar (yellow).
الغواصة لونها أصفر.

City – Madineh مدينة

Village – Day3a ضيعة
House - Beit بيت
Home – Beit بيت
Apartment – Che22a شقة
Tower – Berej برج
Building – Bineye بناية
Skyscraper – Nat7it Sa7eb ناطحة سحاب
Neighborhood – 7ayy حي
Office building – Bineyit Maketib بناية مكاتب

Is this a city or a village?
Hayde madineh aw day3a?
هيدي مدينة أو ضيعة؟

Does he live in a house or an apartment?
Bi3ish (does he live) bi beit aw bi che22a?
بعيش ببيت أو بشقة؟

These skyscrapers are located in the new part of the city.
Hawli nat7et el sa7eb ma7allon bl mayle el jdide men el mdineh.
هولي ناطحات السحاب محلن بالميلة الجديدة من المدينة.

The tower is tall but the building beside it is very short.
El berej tawil (tall) bas el bineye yelli 7ado (beside) ktir 2asira.
البرج طويل بس البناية يلي حده كتير قصيرة.

This is a historical neighborhood.
Hayda 7ayy terikhi (historical).
هيدا حي تاريخي.

There is a fence around the construction site.
Fi siyej 7awalen (around) warchet el 3amar.
في سياج حولين ورشة العمار.

Post office – Maktab Barid مكتب بريد
Location – Maw2a3 موقع
Elevator – Ascenseur أسنسير
Stairs – Daraj درج
Fence – Siyej سياج
Construction site – Warchet 3amar ورشة عمار
Bridge – jesr جسر
Gate – Bouwebe بوابة
City hall – Baladiye بلدية
The mayor – Ra2is El Baladiye رئيس البلدية
Fire department – Dife3 Madani دفاع مدني
Fireman - 2etfa2e اطفائي

This residential building does not have an elevator, just stairs.
Hayde el bineye el sakaniye (residential) mafiya (doesn't have) ascenseur, bas fiya daraj.
هيدي البناية السكنية ما فيا أسنسير بس فيا درج.

The post office is located in that office building.
Maktab el barid mawjood bi bineyit el maketib.
مكتب البريد موجود ببناية المكاتب.

The bridge is closed today.
El jesr msakkar lyom.
الجسر مسكّر اليوم.

The gate is open.
El bouwebe maftou7a.
البوابة مفتوحة.

The fire department is located in the building next to city hall.
El dife3 el madani bl bineye yelli 7ad el baladiye.
الدفاع المدني بالبناية الي حد البلدية.

Street – Cheri3 شارع
Main street – Cheri3 Ra2ise شارع رئيسي
Parking – Maw2if موقف
Parking lot – Maw2if موقف
To Park – Ywa2if يوقف
Sidewalk – Rsif رصيف
Traffic – 3aj2at seir عجقة سير
Traffic light - 2ichart El Ser إشارة السير
Red light – 2ichara Hamra إشارة حمرا
Yellow light – 2ichara Safra إشارة صفرا
Green light – 2ichara Khadra إشارة خضرا
Pedestrians - Moushet مشاة
Crosswalk – Mamar Lal Mouchet ممر للمشاة

Parking is on the main street and not on the sidewalk.
El maw2if bl cheri3 el ra2ise mech (not) 3al rsif.
الموقف بالشارع الرئيسي مش عالرصيف.
Where is the parking lot?
Wen el maw2if?
وين الموقف؟
The traffic is very bad today.
El 3aj2a ktir awiye (bad) lyom.
العجقة كتير قوية اليوم.
I don't like to drive on the highway.
Ma-b7eb (I don't like) sou2 3al autostrad.
ما بحب سوق عالأتوستراد.
At a red light you need to stop, at a yellow light you must be prepared to stop and at a green you can drive.
Lezim twa22if 3al 2ichara el hamra, 3al 2ichara el safra lezim tkoun jahiz la twa22if w 3al 2ichara el khadra lezim t2alli3.
لازم توقف عالإشارة الحمرا، عالإشارة الصفرا لازم تكون جاهز لتوقف، وعالإشارة الخضرا لازم تقلع.
This road has too many traffic lights.
Fi ktir 2icharet 3a hayde el tari2.
في كتير إشارات على هيدي الطريق.
Pedestrians use the crosswalk to cross the road.
El mouchet byesta3mlo mamar el mouchet la yo2ta3o (to cross) el tari2.
المشاة بيستعملوا ممر المشاة ليقطعوا الطريق.

Toll lane – Tari2 Bi Rousoum طريق برسوم
Fast lane – Khat El Sari3 خط سريع
Slow lane – Khat El Bati2 خط بطيء
Left lane – Khat El Chmel خط الشمال
Right lane – Khat El Yamin خط اليمين
Highway - Autorstrad اتوستراد
Intersection - Msallabiye مسالابي
Tunnel – Nafa2 نفق
To drive – La Ysou2 ليسوئ
U-turn - Laffe لفة
Shortcut – Tari2 Moukhtasara طريق مختصرة
Stop sign – 2icharet wo2ouf إشارة وقوف

You must avoid the fast lane because it's a toll lane.
Lezim tetjanab (avoid) temchi (to go) 3al khat el sari3 la2enno khat 3aleh rousoum.
لازم تتجنب تمشي عالخط السريع لأنه خط عليه رسوم.

At the intersection, you need to stay in the right lane instead of the left lane because that's a bus lane.
3al msallabiye, lezim tdallak (to stay) 3a khat el yamin badel khat el chmel la2enno lal bas.
عل مسالابي لازم تضلك عخط اليمين بدل خط الشمال لإنه للباص.

The tunnel seems longer than yesterday.
Ka2enno el nafa2 atwal men mberi7 (yesterday).
كإنه النفق أطول من مبيرح.

This is a short drive.
Hayda mechwar 2asir.
هيدا مشوار قصير.

The next bus stop is far away.
M7attet el bas el teni (the next/the second) b3ideh (far).
محطة الباص التاني بعيدة.

You need to turn right at the stop sign and then continue on straight.
Lezim tlef (to turn) 3al yamin 3a 2icharet el wou2ouf w ba3den betkaffe deghri (straight).
لازم تلف عاليمين عإشارة الوقوف وبعدين بتكفي دغري.

Capital – 3asme عاصمة
Resort – Mountaja3 منتجع
Port – Marfa2 مرفئ
Road – Tari2 طريق
Trail – Mamcha ممشى
Bus station – M7attet bas محطة باص
Bus stop – Maw2af Baset موقف باصات
Night club – Malha laili ملهى ليلي
Night club - Night نيت
Downtown – Downtown داون تاون

The capital is a major attraction point for tourists.
El 3asme no2ta jezbe lal souwe7.
.العاصمة نقطة جذابة للسياح

The resort is next to the port.
El montaja3 7ad el marfa2.
.المنتجع حد المرفئ

The night club is located in the downtown district.
El night mawjood bl downtown.
.النيت موجود بالداون تاون

This statue is a city monument.
Hayda el temsel houwe nasb tezkari lal mdineh.
.هيدا التمثال هوي نصب تزكاري للمدينة

You need to follow the trail alongside the main street to reach the bus station.
Lezim tel7a2 el mamcha elli 3a-janb (alongside) el tari2 el ra2ise ta tousal (to reach) 3a m7attet el bas.
.لازم تلحق الممشى اللي عجنب الطريق الرئيسي تتوصل عمحطة الباص

District – Manti2a منطقة
County - Mou2ata3a مقاطعة
Statue – Temsel تمثال
Monument – Nasb Tezkari نصب تزكاري
Castle – 2al3a قلعة
Palace - 2ser قصر
Cathedral – Katedra2iye كاتدرائية
Zoo – 7ade2it el 7aywanat حديقة الحيوانات
Science museum – Mat7af El 3ouloum متحف العلوم
Playground – Mal3ab ملعب
Swimming pool – Piscine بسين
Jail / prison – 7abs حبس

This is an ancient castle.
Hayde 2al3a adimeh (ancient).
هيدي قلعة قديمة.

That is a beautiful cathedral.
Hayde katedra2iye 7elwe.
هيدي كاتدرائية حلوة.

Do you want to go to the zoo or the science museum?
Badak (do you want) trou7 3a-7ade2it el 7aywanat aw 3a mat7af el 3ouloum?
بدك تروح عحديقة الحيوانات أو عمتحف العلوم؟

The children are in the playground.
El wled bl mal3ab.
الأولاد بالملعب.

The swimming pool is closed for the community today.
El piscine msakara (closed) lyom lal 3alam.
البسين مسكرة اليوم للعالم.

The jail in this county is very small.
El 7abs ktir zghir bhal balad.
الحبس كتير صغير بهالبلد.

Entertainment - Tesleye تسلية

Movie – Film فلم
Theater (movie theater) – Cinéma سنيما
Actor – Moumasil ممثل
Actress – Moumasileh ممثلة
Genre – No3 نوع
Subtitles – Tarjame ترجمة
Action – Action أكشن
Foreign – 2ajnabe أجنبي
Mystery – Leghez لغز
Suspense – Techwi2 تشويق

There are three new movies at the theater that I want to watch.
Fi tlet aflam jdidi bl cinema 7ebbe e7daron (to watch).
في تلات أفلام جديدة بالسنيما حابة أحضرون.

He is a really good actor.
Houwe moumasil kteer chater.
هوي ممثل كتير شاطر.

She is an excellent actress.
Hiye moumassileh chatra ktir.
هي ممثلة شاطرة كتير.

That was a good action movie.
Ken film action 7elo.
كان فلم أكشن حلو.

I need subtitles if I watch a foreign film.
Badi tarjame iza badi e7dar film 2ajnabe.
بدي ترجمة إزا بدي أحضر فلم أجنبي.

Films of the mystery-suspense genre are usually good movies.
Aflam men no3 el-leghez wa el-techwi2 henne floume 7elwe.
أفلام من نوع اللغز و التشويق هنه فلومي حلوة.

Documentary – Wasa2iki وثائقي
Biography – Sireh Chakhsiyeh سيرة شخصية
Drama – Drama دراما
Comedy – Comedy كوميدي
Romance – Romanci رومنسي
Horror – Ro3ob رعب
Animation - Animation أنيميشن
Cartoon – Cartoon كرتون
Director – (m) Moukhrij مخرج
Director – (f) Moukhrijeh مخرجة
Producer - (m) Mountij منتج
Producer - (f) Mountijeh منتجة
Audience – Joumhour جمهور

I like documentary films. However, comedy-drama or romance films are better.
B7eb el floume el wasa2ikiyeh. Bas aflam el-comedy-drama aw romance a7la.
بحب الفلومي الوثائقية بس أفلام الكوميدي دراما أو الرومنسي أحلى.

Sometimes biographies are boring to watch.
2aw2et (sometimes) floumet el siyar el chakhsiye bizah2o (boring).
أوقات أفلام السير الشخصية بزهقوا.

My favorite genre of movies are the horror movies.
No3 el floume el mouffaddal 3andi (of mine) henne el ro3ob.
نوع الفلومي المفضل عندي هني الرعب.

It's fun to watch animated movies.
Floumet el animation bisallo lama to7daron.
فلومت الأنيميشن بسلوا لما تحضرون.

The director and the producer can meet the audience today.
El moukhrij wel mountij fiyon (they can) yelte2o (to meet) bl joumhour lyom.
المخرج والمنتج فيون يلتقوا بالجمهور اليوم.

Entertainment – Tesleye تسلية
Television – Television تليفيجين
A show (as in television) – Bernemij برنامج
A show (as in live performance) – El 3ared العرض
Channel – M7atta المحطة
Series – Mousalsal المسلسل
Commercial – Di3aye دعاية
Episode – 7al2a حلقة
Screen – Cheche شاشة
Camera – Camera كاميرا
Script – Nass نص

It's time to buy a new television.
Sar wa2t nechtri television jdid.
صار وقت نشتري تليفيجين جديد.

This was the first episode of this television show yet it was a long series.
Hayde kenit awal 7al2a men hayda el bernemij ma3 2enno (although) kan mousalsal tawil ktir.
هيدي كانت أول حلقة من هيدا البرنامج مع إنه كان مسلسل طويل كتير.

There aren't any commercials on this channel.
Ma fi ay di3ayet 3ala hal m7atta.
ما في أي دعاية على هالمحطة.

We want to enjoy the entertainment tonight.
Badna netsalla el layle.
بدنا نتسلى الليلة.

I must read my script in front of the screen and the camera
Lezim e2ra (to read) el nass taba3i m2ebil el checheh wel camera.
لازم إقرا النص تبعي مقابل الشاشه والكاميرا.

Anchorman – Mouzi3 مذيع
Anchorwoman – Mouzi3a مذيعة
News – Akhbar أخبار
News station – M7attet Akhbar محطة أخبار
Screening – Projection بروجيكشن
Live – Moubachar مباشر
Broadcast – Bath بث
Headlines – Al 3anewin العناوين
Viewer – (m) Mouchehid مشاهد
Viewer – (f) Mouchehideh مشاهدة
Speech – Khoutab خطاب

This anchorman and anchorwoman work for our local news station.
Hayda el mouzi3 wel mouzi3a byechteghlo (work) bi m7attet el akhbar taba3na.
هيدا المذيع والمذيعة بشتغلوا بمحطة الأخبار تبعنا.

They decided to screen a live broadcast on the news.
2araro (they decided) ybetho bath moubachar 3al akhbar.
قرروا يبثوا بث مباشر عالأخبار.

The news station featured the headlines before the program began.
M7attet el akhbar 3aradit (featured) el 3anewin abel ma yballach (began) el bernemij.
محطة الاخبار عرضت العناوين قبل ما يبلش البرنامج.

Tonight, all the details about the incident were mentioned on the news.
Il-layleh, zakarou (mentioned/reminded) kel tafasil el hadis (incident) 3al akhbar.
الليلة ذكروا كل تفاصيل الحادث عالأخبار.

The viewers wanted to hear the presidential speech today.
El mouchehidin ken baddon yesma3ou (to hear) khoutab el ra2is (presidential) lyom.
المشاهدين كان بدن يسمعوا خطاب الرئيس اليوم.

Theater (play) – Masra7iyeh مسرحية
A musical play – Masra7iyeh Ghine2iyeh مسرحية غنائية
A play – Masra7iyeh مسرحية
Theater stage – Masra7 مسرح
Audition – Ade2 أداء
Performance – 3ared عرض
Box office – Box office بوكس أوفس
Ticket – Tazkara تذكرة
Singer – Moughanni مغني
Singer – (f) Moughanniyeh مغنية
Band – Fer2a فرقة
Orchestra – Orchestra ألكسترا
Opera – Opera أوبيرا

It was a great musical performance.
Ken el 3ared el mousi2i ktir 7elou?
كان العرض الموسيقي كتير حلو.

Can I audition for the play on this stage?
Fyi addim ade2 lal masra7iyeh 3al haida el-masra7?
فيي أقدم أداء للمسرحية على هيدا المسرح؟

She is the lead singer of the band.
Hyeh el moughanniyeh el ra2isyeh (main) taba3 el fer2a.
هي المغنية الرئيسية تبع الفرقة.

I will go to the box office tomorrow to purchase tickets for the opera.
Ra7 rou7 3al box office boukra la echtri tazaker lal opera.
رح روح على البوكس أوفس بكرا لإشتري تذاكر للأوبيرا.

The orchestra needs to perform below the stage.
El orchestra badda t2addim el 3ared men ta7et el masra7.
اللكسترا بدا تقدم العرض من تحت المسرح.

Music – Mousi2a موسيقى
Song – Ghenniyeh غنية
Musical instrument – 2ele Mousi2iyeh آلة موسيقية
Musical instrument – Adawet el mousi2iyeh أدوات موسيقية
Drum – Tambour طمبور
Guitar – Guitar غيتار
Piano – Piano بيانو
Trumpet – Trompette ترمبوت
Violin – Violon فيولن
Flute – Flûte فلوت
Art – Fann فن
Gallery – Ma3rad معرض
Studio – Studio ستوديو
Museum – Mat7af متحف

I like to listen to this type of music. I hope to hear a good song.
Bhebb esma3 no3 (type) el mousi2a hayda. Betmanna esma3 ghenniyeh 7elweh.
.بحب اسمع نوع الموسيقى هيدي. بتمنى اسمع غنية حلوة

The common musical instruments that are used in a concert are drums, guitars, pianos, trumpets, violins, and flutes.
El adawet el mousi2iyeh yali 3adatan (common/normal) byesta3mlouwa bel 7aflat henneh el tabel, el guitar, el piano, el trompette, el violon wel flute.
الأدوات الموسيقية يلي عادةً بيستعملوها بالحفلات هيني الطبل، الغيتار، البيانو، التروبت والفيول والفلوت.

The art gallery has a studio for rent.
Ma3rad el-fan 3ando (has) studio lal 2ajar.
.معرض الفن عنده استديو للإيجار

I went to an art museum yesterday.
Re7et 3ala met7af lal fann mberi7.
.رحت على متحف للفن مبيرح

Food - Akel أكل

Grocery store - Dekken دكان
Market - Dekken دكان
Supermarket – Supermarket سوبر ماركت
Groceries - Charcuterie شاركوتيري
Butcher shop – Mal7ameh ملحمة
Butcher – Le77am لحام
Bakery - Foron فرن
Baker - Farran فران
Breakfast – Terwi2a ترويقة
Lunch – Ghada غدا
Dinner – 3acha عشا
Meat – La7meh لحمه
Chicken – Djej جاج

Where is the nearest grocery store?
Wen a2rab (nearest) dekken?
وين أقرب دكان؟

Where can I buy meat and chicken?
Wen fyi echtri la7meh w djej?
وين فيي أشتري لحمة وجاج؟

The groceries are already in the car.
El charcuterie aslan (already) bel siyara.
الشاركوتيري أصلاً بالسيارة.

The butcher shop is near the bakery.
El mal7ameh had el foron.
الملحمة حد الفرن.

I have to go to the market, to buy a half kilo of meat.
Lezim rou7 3al dekken, la echtri noss (half) kilo la7meh.
لازم روح عالدكان لإشتري نص كيلو لحمة.

Seafood – Simar el Ba7er سمار البحر
Egg – Beid بيض
Milk – 7alib حليب
Cheese - Jebneh جبنة
Butter – Zebdeh زبدة
Bread – Khebez خبز
Oil – Zeit زيت
Flour – Ta7in طحين
Baked – Makhbouz مخبوز
Cake – Cake كيك
Beer - Bira بيره
Wine – Mbid امبيد
Cinnamon – 2erfeh قرفه
Powder – Boudra بودرة
Mustard – Khardal خردل

For lunch, we can eat seafood, and then pasta for dinner.
Fina (we can) nekol simar ba7er 3al ghada w ba3den ma3karoneh 3al 3acha.
فينا ناكل سمار بحر عالغدا وبعدين معكرونة عالعشا.

I usually eat bread with cheese for breakfast.
3adatan bekol khebez ma3 jebneh 3al terwi2a.
عادةً باكل خبز مع جبنة عالترويقة.

I don't have any ketchup or mustard to put on my hotdog.
Ma 3andi ketchup aw khardal la 7ott 3al hotdog.
ما عندي كاتشاب أو خردل لحط عالهوت دوغ.

I need to buy flour, eggs, milk, butter, and oil to bake a cake.
Lezim echtri ta7in, beid, 7alib, zebdeh, w zeit ta ekhboz cake.
لازم أشتري طحين، بيض، زبدة، وزيت تا أخبز الكيك.

On which aisle is the cinnamon powder?
Bi aya saff (aisle) ble2i (find) el 2erfeh el boudra?
بأي صف بلاقي القرفة البودرة؟

Where can I buy beer and wine.
Wen fyi echtri bira w mbid.
وين فيي أشتري بيره وأمبيد.

Menu – Menu منيو
Beef – La7meh لحمة
Lamb – kharoof خاروف
Pork – Khanzir خنزير
Steak – Bifteck بيفتك
Hamburger – Hamburger همبرجر
Water – Mayy ماي
Salad – Sala9a سلطة
Soup – Chawraba شوربة
Appetizer – Mou2abbilet مقبلات

Do you have a menu in English?
3andak menu 2englizi?
عندك منيو إنجليزي؟

Which is preferable, the fried fish or the grilled lamb?
Shou betfaddil (preferable), el samak el ma2li aw la7em el-kharoof el-mechwi?
شو بتفضّل السمك المقلي أو لحم الخاروف المشوي؟

I want to order a cup of water, a soup for my appetizer, and pizza for my entrée.
Badi otlob kebbeyit (cup) may, w chawraba ka-mou2abilet, w pizza lal teblicheh.
بدي أطلب كوباية ماي، وشوربة كمقبلات، وبيتزا للتبليشي.

I want to order a steak for myself, a hamburger for my son, and ice cream for my wife.
Badi otlob steak la eli, hamburger la ebni, w bouza la marti.
بدي أطلب ستيك لإلي، همبرجر لإبني، بوظة لمرتي.

Which type of dessert is included with my coffee?
Shou no3 el 7alawiyet yali byeji ma3 el 2ahweh?
شو نوع الحلويات اللي بيجي مع القهوة؟

Cooked - Matboukh مطبوخ
Boiled – Maslou2 مسلوق
Fried – Me2li مقلي
Grilled - Mechwi مشوي
Broiled – Maslou2 مسلوق
Raw – Nayy نيّ
Dessert – 7alawiyet حلويات
Ice cream – Bouza بوظة
Coffee – 2ahweh قهوة
Olive oil – Zet Zaytoun زيت زيتون
Fish – Samak سمك
Juice – 3aseer عصير
Tea – Chay شاي
Honey – 3asal عسل
Sugar – Sekkar سكر

Can I order a salad with a hard boiled egg and olive oil on the side?
Fyi otlob salata ma3 beid maslou2 w zet zaytoun 7addo?
فيي أطلب سلطة مع بيض مسلوق وزيت زيتون حدو؟

Is the piece of fish in the sushi cooked or raw?
Cha2fit el samak yali bel sushi matboukha aw nayyeh?
شقفة السمك يلي بالسوشي مطبوخة أو نيّة؟

I want to order a fruit juice instead of a soda.
Badi otlob 3aseer badel (instead) el pepsi.
بدي أطلب عصير بدل البيبسي.

I want to order tea with a teaspoon of honey instead of sugar.
Badi otlob chay ma3 mel3a2it 3asal badel el sekkar.
بدي أطلب شاي مع ملعقة عسل بدل السكر.

The tip is 20% at this restaurant.
El tips 3echrin bel-miyeh (percent) bi hayda el mat3am.
التبس عشرين بالمية بهيدا المطعم.

Vegetarian - Nabati نباتي
Vegetarian - (f) Nabatiyeh نباتية
Vegan – Nabati نباتي
Vegan – (f) Nabatiyeh نباتية
Dairy – Alben w Ajben ألبان وأجبان
Dairy products – Mantoojat Alben w Ajben منتجات ألبان وأجبان
Salt – Mele7 ملح
Pepper – Fulful فلفل
Flavor – Nak-ha نكهة
Spices – Bharat بهارات
Rice – Rezz رز
Fries – Batata بطاطا
Nuts – 2loubeit قلوبات
Peanuts – Festo2 فستق

I don't eat meat because I am a vegetarian.
Ma bekol la7meh la2enni nabati.
ما باكل لحمه لأني نباتي.

My brother won't eat dairy products because he is a vegan.
Khayi ma byekol alben w ajben la2enno nabati.
خيي ما باكل الألبان أو الأجبان لأنه نباتي.

Food tastes much better with salt, pepper, and other spices.
Ta3mit (taste) el akel a7san bi ktir ma3 mele7, fulful, w gher bharat.
طعمة الأكل أحسن بكتير مع ملح، فلفل وغير بهارات.

It's healthier to eat rice instead of fries.
So77i aktar tekol rezz badeil batata.
صحّي أكتر تاكل رز بدل بطاطا.

I want to try a sample of that piece of cheese.
Hebib jarrib cha2feh men ot3it (piece) el jebneh haydik.
حابب جرّب شقفة من قطعة الجبنة هيديك.

I have allergies to nuts and peanuts.
3andi 7asesyeh min el-2loubeit wel festo2.
عندي حساسية من القلوبات والفستق.

Soy – Soya صويا
Sauce – Salsa صلصة
Sandwich – Sandwich ساندوش
Mayonnaise – Mayonnaise ميونيز
Jelly – Jello جيلو
Chocolate - Chocolat شوكليت
Cookies - Biscuit بسكيت
Candy – Bonbon بنبون
Whipped cream – Crème fraiche كريمي فريش
Popsicle – Bouzit Talej بوظة تلج
Frozen - Mjallad مجلد
Thawed – Deyib دايب

This sauce is disgusting.
Hal salsa me2erfeh.
هالصلصة مقرفة.

Why do you always put mayonnaise on your sandwich?
Lech deyman (always) bet7ott mayonnaise bi sandwichtak?
ليه دايماً بتحط ميونيز بساندويشتك؟

The food is still frozen so we need to wait for it to thaw.
El akel ba3do mjallad fa lezim nentor (to wait) la ydoub.
الأكل بعده مجلّد فلازم ننطر ليدوب.

Please bring me a bowl of cereal and a slice of toasted bread with jelly.
3mol-ma3rouf (please) jebli (bring) kesit cornflakes w cha2fit khebez toast ma3 jello.
اعمل معروف جبلي كاسة كورنفلكس و شقفة خبز توست مع جيلو.

The only things I have in my freezer are popsicles.
Al chaghleh (things) el wa7ideh yali 3andi bel tellejeh hiyeh bouzet el talej.
الشغلة الوحيدة يلي عندي بالتلاجة هيي بوظة التلج.

No chocolate, candy, or whipped cream until after dinner.
Ma fi, la chocolat, la bonbon w la crème fraiche la ba3d el 3acha.
ما في لا شوكولاته لا بنبون لا كريمة فريش لبعد العشا.

Vegetables – Khodra خضرة

Grilled vegetables – Khodra Mechwiyeh خضرة مشوية
Steamed vegetables – Khodra Maslou2a خضرة مسلوقة
Tomato - Banadoura بندورة
Carrot - Jazra جزر
Lettuce – Khass خس
Radish – Fejel فجل
Beet – Chmandar شمندر
Eggplant – Betenjen بيتنجان
Bell Pepper – Flayfleh فليفلة
Hot pepper – Flayfleh 7arra فليفلة حارة

Grilled vegetables or steamed vegetables are popular side dishes at restaurants.
El khodra el mechwiyeh wel maslou2a bto3tabar (considered) men aktar el s7oun el-janibiyeh cha3biyeh bel-mata3im.
.الخضرة المشوية والمسلوقة بتعتبر من أكثر الصحون الجانبية شعبية بالمطاعم

I put carrots, bell peppers, lettuce, and radishes in my salad.
B7ott jazar, flayfleh, khass, w fejel bel sala9a taba3i.
.بحط جزر، فليفلة، خس وفجل بالسلطة تبعي

It's not hard to grow tomatoes.
Mech ktir so3ob tezra3 banadoura.
.مش كتير صعب تزرع بندورة

Eggplant can be cooked or fried.
Fik (can be) totbokh aw te2li el betenjen.
.فيك تطبخ أو تقلي البيتنجان

I like beets in my salad.
B7ebb el chmandar bel sala9a taba3i.
.بحب الشمندر بالسلطة تبعي

Why are chili peppers so spicy?
Lech el flayfleh el 7arra hal2ad (so) 7arra?
ليش الفليفلة الحمرا هالقد حارة؟

Celery – Krefes كرفس
Spinach – Sbenikh سبانخ
Cabbage – Malfouf ملفوف
Cauliflower – 2arnabit قرنابيط
Beans – Loubiyeh لوبيه
Corn – Dera درة
Garlic - Toum توم
Onion – Basal بصل
Artichoke – Ardi Chawki أرضي شوكي

Celery and spinach have natural vitamins.
El krefes wel sbenikh fiyon vitaminet tabi3iyeh (natural).
الكرفس والسبانخ فيون فيتامينات طبيعية.

Fried cauliflower tastes better than fried cabbage.
El 2arnabit el me2li ta3mto atyab (better) men (than) el malfouf el me2li.
القرنبيط المقلي طعمته أطيب من الملفوف المقلي.

Rice and beans are my favorite side dish.
El fasoulya w rezz atyab akleh 3andi.
الفاصوليا والرز أطيب أكلة عندي.

I like to put butter on corn.
B7ebb 7ott zebdeh 3al dera.
بحب حط زبدة عالدرة.

Garlic is an important ingredient in many cuisines.
El toum moukawwen (ingredient) mhemm (important) bi 3eddit (many) matabekh (cusines).
التوم مكوّن مهم بعدة مطابخ.

Where is the onion powder?
Wen el basal el boudra?
وين البصل البودرة؟

Artichokes are difficult to peel.
El ardi chawki byet2ashar (to peel) bi s3oubeh (difficult).
الأرضي شوكي بيتقشر بصعوبة.

Cucumber – Khyar خيار
Lentils – 3adas عدس
Peas – Bazella بازيلا
Green onion – Basal Akhdar بصل أخضر
Herbs – A3cheib أعشاب
Basil – 7aba2 حبق
Cilantro – Kezbra كزبرة
Dill - Chabet شبت
Parsley – Ba2dounis بقدونس
Mint – Na3na3 نعنع
Vegetable garden – Jnaynet Khodra جنينة خضرة

I want to order lentil soup.
Badi otlob chawrabit 3adas.
بدي أطلب شوربة عدس.

Please put the green onion in the refrigerator.
3mol ma3rouf 7ott el basal el akhdar bel berrad.
اعمل معروف حط البصل الأخضر بالبراد.

The most common kitchen herbs are basil, cilantro, dill, parsley, and mint.
Aktar a3sheib btosta3mal bel matbakh hiyeh el 7aba2, el kezbra, el chabet, el ba2dounis, wel na3na3.
أكتر أعشاب بتستعمل بالمطبخ هييه الحبق، الكزبرة، الشبت، البقدونس والنعنع.

The potatoes in the field are ready to harvest.
El batata yali bel 7a2leh sarou jehzin la yet7awwashou.
البطاطا يلي بالحقلة صاروا جاهزين ليتحوشوا.

The tomatoes are fresh but the cucumbers are rotten.
El banoudarat 9aza bass el khyarat m3afnin (rotten).
البندورات طازة بس الخيارات معفنين.

I must water my vegetable garden.
Lezim 2os2i jnaynit el khodra taba3i.
لازم أسقي جنينة الخضرة تبعي.

Potato – Batata بطاطا
Sweet Potato – Batata 7elweh بطاطا حلوة
Mushroom – Champignon شابقنون
Asparagus – Hiliuwn هليون
Seaweed – A3cheib Ba7riyeh أعشاب بحرية
Pumpkin – Ya2tin يقطين
Squash – 2are3 قرع
Zucchini – Kousa كوسا
Chick peas – 7ommos حمص

Some of the most common vegetables for tempura are sweet potatoes and mushrooms.
El khedra yali byesta3emlouwa aktar chi bel tempura henneh el batata el helweh wel champignon.
.الخضرة يلي بيستعملوها أكتر شي بالتمبورة هني البطاطا الحلوة والشابقنون

I want to order vegetarian sushi with asparagus and cucumber along with a side of seaweed salad.
Badi otlob sushi vegetarian ma3 hiliuwn w khiyar w 7addon sala9it a3cheib ba7riyeh.
.بدي أطلب سوشي فيجيترين مع هليون وخيار وحدن سلطة أعشاب بحرية

I enjoy eating pumpkin seeds as a snack.
B7ebb ekol bezer (small seed) el la2tin metel (as a/like a) snack.
.بحب آكل بزر اليقطين متل السناك

Chickpeas are a popular ingredient in Middle Eastern food.
El 7ommos men el moukawwinet el aktar cha3biyeh bi akel el-chare2 el 2awsat.
.الحمص من المكونات الأكتر شعبية بأكل الشرق الأوسط

Is there Zucchini in the soup?
Fi kousa bel chawraba?
في كوسا بالشوربة؟

I like to put ginger dressing on my salad.
B7eb 7ott zanjabil 3ala-el (on the) sala9a taba3i.
.بحب أحط زنجبيل على السلطة تبعي

Fruits – Fwekeh فواكه

Apple – Teffe7 تفاح
Banana – Moz موز
Orange – Berd2en بردقان
Grapefruit – Grapefruit جريب فروت
Peach – Derre2 دريق
Tropical fruit – Fawekeh estiwe2iyeh فواكة استوائية
Papaya - Papaya بابايا
Coconut – Jawz el hened جوز هند
Cherry – Karaz كرز

Can I add raisins to the apple pie?
Fyi 7ot zbib 3ala el tart (pie) el tefe7?
فيي حط زبيب على تورتة التفاح؟

Orange juice is a wonderful source of Vitamin C.
3asir el berd2en masdar (source) mumtaz lal vitamin c.
عصير البردقان مصدر ممتاز للفيتامين سي.

Grapefruits are extremely beneficial for your health.
El grapefruit ktir bi fid (benificial) el so77a.
الجريب فروت كتير بفيد الصحة.

I have a peach tree in my front yard.
3andi chajrit derre2 bel sa7ah elli eddem (in front) el bet.
عندي شجرة دراق اللي بالساحة قدام البيت.

I bought papayas and coconuts at the supermarket to prepare a tropical fruit salad.
Chtrit papaya w jawz (large seed) el hened men el supermarket la a3mol saltit fawekeh estiwe2i.
شريت بابايا وجوز الهند من السوبرماركت لإعمل سلطة فواكة استوائية.

I want to travel to Japan to see the famous cherry blossom.
Baddi sefir 3al yaban la shouf (to see) zhour (blossom) el karaz el machhoura (famous).
بدي سافر عاليابان لشوف زهور الكرز المشهورة.

Bananas are tropical fruits.
El moz fweki 2istiwe2iyeh.
الموز فواكة استوائية.

Raisins – Zbib زبيب
Prunes - Khokh خوخ
Dates – Bala7 بلح
Figs – Tin تين
Fruit salad – Saltit fawekeh سلطة فواكة
Dried fruit – Fawekeh Mjaffafeh فواكة مجففة
Apricot – Mechmoch مشمش
Pear – Njas انجاص
Avocado – Avocat أفوكاد
Ripe – Mestwi مستوي

I want to mix dates and figs in my fruit salad.
Badi ekhlot bala7 w tin bi saltiti el-fawekeh .
.بدي أخلط بلح وتين بسلطتي الفواكة

Apricots and prunes are my favorite dried fruits.
El mechmoch wel khokh henneh el fweki el mjaffaffeh (dried) el mfaddaleh 3andi.
.المشمش والخوخ هني الفواكة المجففة المفضلة عندي

Pears are delicious.
El njas tayyib (delicious).
.النجاص طيّب

The avocados aren't ripe yet.
El avocat ma stawa (ripe) ba3ed.
.الأفوكادو ما استوى بعد

The green apple is very sour.
El teffe7 el akhdar ktir 7amid (sour).
.التفاح الأخضر كتير حامض

The unripe peach is usually bitter.
El derre2 yali manno-mestwi (unripe) bi koun morr (bitter) 3adatan.
.الدراق يلي مانه مستوي بكون مر عادةً

Fruit tree – Chajrit Fweki شجرة فواكة
Citrus – 7omdiyet حمضيات
Lemon – 7amod حامض
Lime – 7amod Akhdar حامض أخضر
Pineapple – Ananas أناناس
Melon - Chemmem شمام
Watermelon – Battikh بطيخ

How much does the watermelon juice cost?
Addech 7a22o 3asir (juice) el battikh?
قديش حقه عصير البطيخ؟

I have a pineapple plant inside a pot.
3andi chatlit (a plant) ananas hateta bel wa3a.
عندي شتلة أناناس حطيتا بالوعاء.

Melons grow on the ground.
El chemmem byotla3 3al ared.
الشمام بيطلع عالأرض.

I am going to the fruit-tree section of the nursery today to purchase a few citrus trees.
Lyom badi rou7 3ala matra7 ma bi bi3ou chajar fweki bel machtal (nursery) la echtri chajar 7awamid.
اليوم بدي روح على مطرح ما ببيعوا شجر فواكة بالمشتل لإشتري شجر حوامض.

Plums are seasonal fruits.
El khokh fweki mawsamiyeh (seasonal).
الخوخ فواكة موسمية.

I want to add either lemon juice or lime juice to my salad.
Badi 7ot ya laymoon ya 7amod akhdar 3al sala9a taba3i (my).
بدي حط يا ليمون يا حامض أخضر عالسلطة تبعي.

Strawberry – Fraise فريز
Berry – Tout توت
Raspberry – Tout 3elle2 توت عليق
Blueberry – Tout Azra2 توت أزرق
Grapes – 3eneb عنب
Pomegranate – Remmen رمان
Plum – Khokh خوخ
Olive – Zaytoun زيتون
Grove – Bestein بستان

Strawberries grow during the Spring.
El fraise byotla3 (grow) bel rabi3 (spring).
.الفريز بيطلع بالربيع

There are many raspberries growing on the bush.
Fi ktir tout 3elle2 tal3in (hanging) 3al chajra (bush).
.في كتير توت عليق طالعين عالشجرة

Blueberry juice is very sweet.
3asir el tout el azra2 (blue) ta3emto (its taste) ktir 7elweh.
.عصير التوت الأزرق طعمته كتير حلوة

Berries are acidic fruits.
El tout byo3tabar (considered) men el fweki el 7amda (acidic).
.التوت بعتبر من الفواكة الحامضة

Pomegranate juice contains a very high level of antioxidants.
3asir el remmen fyo kammyeh kbireh men moudaddet (level/amount) el axadeh.
.عصير الرمان فيه كمية كبيرة من مضادات الأكسدة

I need to pick the grapes to make the wine.
Badi 2o2tof (to pick) el 3eneb la a3mol mbid.
.بدي أقطف العنب لأعمل أمبيد

I have an olive grove in my backyard.
3endi besten (grove) zaytoun bi jnaynti.
.عندي بستان زيتون بالجنينة

Shopping – Tasawu2 تسوق

Clothes – Tyeb تياب
Clothing store – Ma7al tyeb محل تياب
For sale – Lal Be3 للبيع
Hat – Bornayta برنيطة
Shirt – 2amis قميص
Shoes – Sebbat سباط
Skirt - Tannoura تنورة
Dress – Festan فستان
Pants – Bantalon بنطلون
Shorts – Short شورت

There are a lot of clothes for sale today.
Fi ktir tyeb lal-be3 (for sale) lyom.
.في كتير تياب للبيع اليوم

Does this hat look good?
Chakl hayde el bornayta meni7?
شكل هيدي البرنيطة منيح؟

I am happy with this shirt and these shoes.
Ana mabsout (happy) bi hayde el 2amise wel sebbat.
.أنا مبسوط بهيدي القميص والسباط

She prefers a skirt instead of a dress.
Hyeh betfaddil tannoura badal-men (more than) festan.
.هي بتفضل تنورة بدل من فستان

These pants aren't my size.
Hayda el bantalon mech (aren't) 3a 2yesi.
.هيدا البنطلون مش عقياسي

Suit – Badleh بدلة
Vest - Gilet جيليه
Tie – Cravatte غرفتيه
Uniform – Badleh بدلة
Belt – 2chat قشاط
Socks – Kalset كلسات
Gloves – Kfouf كفوف
Glasses – 3waynet عوينات
Sunglasses – 3waynet chames عوينات شمس
Size – 2yes قياس
Small - Zghir صغير
Small - (f) zghireh صغيرة
Medium - Wasat وسط
Large – Kbeer كبير
Thick - Smik سميك
Thin – R2i2 رقيق
Thrift store – Ma7al Beleh محل البالة

Where can I find a thrift store? I want to buy a suit, a vest, and a tie.
Wen fiyi le2i ma7al beleh? Badi echtri badleh, gilet w cravatte.
وين فيي لاقي محل بالة؟ بدي أشتري بدلة، جيليه وغرفتيه.

There are uniforms for school at the clothing store.
Fi badlet lal madraseh bi ma7al el tyeb.
في بدلات للمدرسة بمحل التياب.

I forgot my socks, belt, and shorts at your house.
Nsit kalseti, 2chati w shorti 3andak bel bet.
نسيت كلساتي و قشاطي وشورتي عندك بالبيت.

These gloves are a size too small. Do you have a medium size?
Hawdeh el kfouf 2yeson ktir zghir. Fi 3andak 2yes wasat?
هودي الكفوف قياسن كتير صغير. في عندك قياس وسط؟

Today I don't need my reading glasses. I only need my sunglasses.
Lyom manni me3tez 3waynet el 2reyeh. Bass 3eyiz 3waynet el chames.
اليوم ماني معتاز عوينات القراية، بس عايز عوينات الشمس.

Jacket – Jacket جاكيت
Scarf - Écharpe إيشارب
Mittens – Kfouf كفوف
Sleeve – Kemm كم
Boots (rain, winter) – Boots بوتس
Sweater – Kanzeh كنزة
Bathing suit – Maioh مايوه
Flip flops – Mecheyeh Bi Osba3 مشاية بإصبع
Tank top – Top توب
Sandals – Sandales صندل

We are going to the mountain today so don't forget your jacket, mittens, and scarf.
Lyom ray7in 3al jabal fa ma tensa jackettak, el kfouf wel echarpe.
اليوم راحين عالجبل فما تنسى جكيتك، الكفوف والإيشارب.

I have long sleeve shirts and short sleeve shirts.
3andi 2omsan kemm tawil w kemm 2asir.
عندي قمصان كم طويل وكم قصير.

Boots and sweaters are meant for winter.
El boots wel kalset ma3moulin lal cheteh.
البوتس والكلسات معمولين للشتا.

At the beach, I wear a bathing suit and flip flops.
3al ba7er, belbos (to wear) maioh w mecheyeh bi osba3.
عالبحر بلبس مايوه و مشاية بإصبع.

I want to buy a tank top for summer.
Badi echtri top lal sayf-iyeh (summer).
بدي أشتري توب للصيفية.

Heels – Ka3eb كعب
On sale – Tanzeelat تنزيلات
Expensive – Ghali غالي
Free – Bi-balech ببلاش
Discount - Khasem خصم
Discount - Mwa2finon موئفنن
Cheap – Rkhis رخيص
Shopping – Tasawu2 تسوّق
Mall – Mall مول

I can't wear heels on the beach, only sandals.
Ma fyi elbos ka3eb 3al ba7er, bass fyi elbos sandal.
ما فيي ألبس كعب عالبحر بس فيي ألبس صندل.

What will be on sale tomorrow?
3a shou fi tanzeelat bourka?
على شو في تنزيلات بكرا؟

This is free.
Hayde bi balech.
هيدا ببلاش.

Even though these colognes and perfumes are discounted, they are still very expensive.
Ma3-enno (even though) hayde el cologna wel 3alehun khasim, bass ba3don ktir ghalyin.
مع أنه هيدي الكوليجة والبرفيم عليهن خصم، بس بعدن كتير غاليين.

These items are very cheap.
Hawdeh el ghrad (items) ktir rkhas.
هودي الأغراض كتير رخاص.

I can go shopping only on weekends.
Fyi rou7 a3mol shopping bass bel weekend.
فيي روح أعمل شوبيغ بس بالويكند.

Is the local mall far?
El mall el ma7alli (local) b3id?
المول المحلي بعيد؟

Store – Ma7al محل
Business hours – Sa3at el Dawem ساعات الدوام
Open – Maftou7 مفتوح
Closed – Msakkar مسكّر
Entrance - Madkhal مدخل
Exit – Makhraj مخرج
Shopping cart / Shopping basket – Kerrayjeh كراجة
Shopping cart / Shopping basket – Salleh سلة
Shopping bag – Kis lal shopping كيس للشوبيغ
Toy store – Ma7al Al3ab محل ألعاب
Toy – Le3beh لعبة

What are your business hours?
Shou henneh se3at el dawem taba3ak?
شو هني ساعات الدوام تبعك؟

What time does the store open?
Ayya-se3a (what time) byefta7 el ma7al?
أي ساعة بيفتح المحل؟

What time does the store close?
Aya se3a bi sakkir el ma7al?
أي ساعة بسكر المحل؟

Where is the entrance?
Wen el madkhal?
وين المدخل؟

Where is the exit?
Wen el makhraj?
وين المخرج؟

My children want to go to the toy store so they can fill up the shopping cart with toys.
Wledi baddon yrou7ou 3a ma7al el al3ab la y3abbou el kerrayjeh 2al3ab.
أولادي بدن يروحوا عمحل الألعاب ليعبوا الكرييجية ألعاب.

I need a large shopping basket when I go to the supermarket.
Badi salleh kbireh wa2et (during the time) rou7 3al supermarket.
بدي سلة كبيرة وقت روح عالسوبرماركت.

Book store – Maktabeh مكتبه
Music store – Ma7al lal mousi2a محل للموسيقى
Jeweler - Jawharji جوهرجي
Jewelry – Moujawharat مجوهرات
Gold - Dehab دهب
Silver - Fodda فضة
Diamond – 2elmaz ألماس
Necklace – 3a2ed عقد
Bracelet - Aswarah أسوارة
Earrings – 7ala2 حلق
Gift – Hdiyeh هدية
Coin – Lira ليرة
Antique – Antika أنتيكا
Dealer – Tejir تاجر

There is a sale at the bookstore right now.
Fi khasim bel maktabeh halla2.
.في خصم بالمكتبه هلأ

It's difficult to find a music store these days.
So3beh tle2i ma7al mousi2a hal 2iyem.
.صعبة تلاقي محل موسيقى هالإيام

The jeweler sells gold and silver.
El jawharji bi bi3 dehab w fodda.
.الجوهرجي ببيع دهب وفضة

I want to buy a diamond necklace.
Badi echtri 3a2ed 2elmaz.
.بدي أشتري عقد ألماس

This bracelet and those pair of earrings are gifts for my daughter.
Hayde el aswarah w joz el 7ala2 hdiyeh (present) men benti.
.هيدي الأسوارة وجوز الحلق هدية من بنتي

He is an antique coin dealer.
Houeh tejir lirat antika.
.هو تاجر ليرات أنتيكا

Family – El 3ayleh العيلة

Mother – 2emm إم
Father – Bayy بي
Son – 2eben ابن
Daughter – Benet بنت
Brother – Khayy خي
Sister – 2ekhet أخت
Husband – Joz جوز
Wife - Mara مرة
Parents – 2ahel أهل
Child – 2eben ابن
Baby – Walad ولد

I have a big family.
3andi 3ayleh kbireh.
عندي عيلة كبيرة.

My brother and sister are here.
Khayyi w 2ekhti hon.
خيي و إختي هون.

The mother and father want to spend time with their child.
El 2emm wel bayy badon y2addou wa2et ma3 wledon.
الإم والبي بدن يقضوا وقت مع أولادن.

He wants to bring his son and daughter.
Bado yjib ma3o 2ebno w bento.
بدو يجيب معه ابنه وبنته.

That man is a good parent.
Haydek el zalameh bayy meni7.
هيديك الزلمة بيّ منيح.

Grandparents – Jdoud جدود
Grandfather – Jedd جد
Grandmother – Sett ست
Grandson – 7afid حفيد
Granddaughter – 7afideh حفيدة
Grandchildren – 2ahfed حفيد
Nephew – 2eben el Khayy ابن الخي
Niece – Bent el 2ekhet بنت الأخت
Cousin - (M) 2eben el 3amm ابن العم
Cousin - (F) Bent el 3amm بنت العم

The grandfather wants to take his grandson to the movie.
El jedd bado yekhod 7afido 3al cinema.
.الجد بدو ياخد حفيدو عالسنيما

The grandmother needs to give her granddaughter money.
El sett bada ta3ti masari la 7afideta.
.الست بدا تعطي مصاري لحفيدتا

The grandparents want to spend time with their grandchildren.
El jdoud baddon y2addou wa2et ma3 a7fedon.
.الجدود بدن يقضوا وقت مع أحفادن

The husband and wife have a new baby.
El mara w jawza 3andon walad jdid.
.المرة وجوزا عندن ولد جديد

I want to go to the park with my niece and nephew.
Badi rou7 3al park ma3 benet 2ekheti w 2eben khayyi.
.بدي روح عالبارك مع بنت إختي وابن خيي

My cousin wants to see his children.
2eben 3ammi bado yshouf wledo.
.ابن عمي بدو يشوف ولاده

Aunt – 3ammeh عمة
Aunt – Kheleh خالة
Uncle – 3amm عم
Uncle – Khal خال
Man – Zalameh زلمة
Woman – Mara مرة
Stepfather – Joz el 2emm جوز إم
Stepmother – Mart Bayy مرت أب
Stepson – Eben El Joz (Eben El Mara) ابن الجوز /ابن المرة
Stepdaughter – Bent El Joz (Bent El Mara) بنت الجوز /بنت المرة
Stepbrother – Khay Men El Emm (El Bayy) خي من الإم /البيّ
Stepsister – 2ekhet Men El Emm (El Bay) أخت من الإم /البيّ
Half-brother - Khay Men El Emm (El Bayy) خي من الإم /البيّ
Half-sister - 2ekhet Men El Emm (El Bay) أخت من الإم /البيّ

My aunt and uncle came to visit.
Eja (came) 3ammi (Kheli) w 3amti (Khalti) zyara.
إجى عمي وعمتي زيارة.

He is their only child.
Houeih 2ebnon el wa7id (only).
هو ابنن الوحيد.

My wife is pregnant with twins.
Marti 7ebleh bi taum.
مرتي حبلة بتوأم.

He is their eldest son.
Houeih 2ebnon el kbir.
هو ابنن الكبير.

The first-born child usually takes on all the responsibilities.
El walad el 2awwal 3adatan byet7ammal kel el mas2ouliyeh (responsibilites).
الولد الأول عادةً بتحمل كل المسؤولية.

She considers her stepson as her real son.
Hyeh bte3tebir eben jawza metel (as/like) 2ebna el 7a2i2i (real).
هي بتعتبر ابن جوزا ابنا الحقيقي.

She is his stepdaughter.
Hyeh benet marto.
هي بنت مرته.

Ancestor – 2aslef أسلاف
Family tree – Chajrit El 3ayleh شجرة العيلة
Generation – Jil جيل
Relative – 2arib قريب
Family member – Fard Men El 3ayleh فرد من العيلة
First born – El Walad El 2awal الولد الأول
Only child – El Walad El Wa7id الولد الوحيد
Twins – Taum توأم
Pregnant – 7ebleh حبلة
Adopted child – Walad Tabanni ولد تبني
Orphan - Yatim يتيم
Orphan - (f) Yatimeh يتيمة
Adult – Beligh بالغ
Neighbor – Jar جار
Neighbor – (f) Jara جارة
Friend – Rfi2 رفيق
Friend – (f) Rfi2a رفيقة
Roommate – Zamil El Sakan زميل سكن

I was able to find all my relatives and ancestors on my family tree.
2deret (I was able to) le2i kell 2raybinni w 2aslefi 3a chajrit el 3ayleh taba3i.
قدرت لاقي كل قرايبي وأسلافي عشجرة العيلة تبعي.

My parents' generation loved disco music.
Jil 2ahli kenou y7ebbou mousi2a el disco.
جيل أهلي كانوا يحبوا موسيقى الديسكو.

Their adopted child was an orphan.
2ebnon yali metbanyino ken yatim.
ابنن يلي متبنينو كان يتيم.

I have a nice neighbor.
3andi jar (m) meni7 /3andi jara(f) meni7a
عندي جار منيح /عندي جارة منيحة

We need to choose a godfather for the baby.
Lezim nna2i 3errab (god father) lal walad.
لازم ننقي عراب للولد.

Human body – Jesm el 2ensen جسم الإنسان

Head – Ras راس
Face – Wejj وج
Eye – 3ein عين
Ear – Dayneh داينة
Nose – Menkhar منخار
Mouth - Temm تم
Lips – Chfef شفايف
Tongue – Lsen لسان
Cheek – Khadd خد
Chin – Da2en دقن

My chin, cheeks, mouth, lips, and eyes are all part of my face.
Da2ni, khdoudi, temmi, chfefi w 3youni kellon jeze2 (parts) men wejji.
داني، خدودي، تمي، شفايفي و عيوني كلن جزء من وجي.

He has small ears.
3andi dinen zghar.
عندي دنين زغار.

I have a cold so my nose, eyes, mouth, and tongue are affected.
Mgarrab men hek menkhari, 3youni, temmi w lseni m2assarin (affected).
مجرّب من هيك منخاري، عيوني، تمي و لساني متأثرين.

The five senses are sight, touch, taste, smell, and hearing.
El 7awes (senses) el khamseh henneh el nazar, el lames, el zo2, el cham wel sama3.
الحواس الخمسه هني النظر، اللمس، الذوق، الشم و السمع.

I am washing my face right now.
3am (I am) ghassil (washing) wejji halla2 (now).
عم غسل وجي هلأ.

She puts makeup on her cheeks and lipstick on her lips.
Bet7ott makeup 3a khdouda w 7omra (lipstick) 3a chfefa.
بتحط ميكب عخدودا، و حمرا عشفايفا.

Neck – Ra2beh رقبة
Throat – 7ale2 حلق
Forehead – Jbin جبين
Eyebrow – 7ejib حاجب
Eyelashes – Rmouch رموش
Hair – Cha3er شعر
Beard – Da2en دقن
Mustache – Chwerib شوارب
Tooth – Snen. سنان

I have a headache.
3andi waja3 ras.
عندي وجع راس.

My eyebrows are too long.
7wejbi ktir twal.
حواجي كتير طوال.

He must shave his beard and mustache.
Lezim ye7lo2 (shave) da2no w chwerbo.
لازم يحلق دقنه و شواربه.

I brush my teeth every morning.
Bfarchi sneni kel sobo7.
بفرشي سناني كل صبح.

Her hair covered her forehead.
Cha3ra ken mghatta (covered) jbina.
شعرا كان مغطي جبينا.

She has a long neck.
Ra2beta tawileh.
رقبتا طويلة.

I have a sore throat.
7al2i nechif.
حلقي ناشف.

Shoulder – Ketef كتف
Chest – Sodor صدر
Arm – 2id إيد
Elbow – Kou3 كوع
Wrist – Ma3sam معصم
Hand – 2id إيد
Palm (of hand) – Kaff كف
Finger – 2esba3 أصبع
Thumb – 2ebham إبهام
Back – Daher ضهر
Leg – 2ejer إجر
Ankle – Ke7il كاحل
Foot – 2ejer إجر
Toe – 2esba3 2ejer اصبع إجر
Joint – Mafsal مفصل
Muscle – 3adal عضل

His chest and shoulders are very muscular.
Sodro w ktefo ktir m3addlin (muscular).
.صدره و كتفه كتير معدلين

I need to strengthen my arms and legs.
Lezim 2awwi 2idayyi w 2ejrayyi.
.لازم أقوي إيدي وإجري

I accidentally hit his wrist with my elbow.
Darabet (hit) me3samo bi kou3i bel ghalat.
.ضربت معصمه بكوعي بالغلط

I have pain in every part of my body especially in my hand, ankle, and back.
3andi waja3 bi kell jesmi khsousi bi 2idi, bi ke7li, w dahri.
.عندي وجع بكل جسمي، بإيدي بكحلي وضهري

I have muscles and joint pain today.
Fi 3andi waja3 3adal w mafasil lyom.
.في عندي وجع عضل ومفاصل اليوم

I need a new bandage for my thumb.
Badi telzi2it-jere7 (bandaid) la 2ebhemi.
.بدي تلزيقات جروح لإبهامي

Belly - Baten بطن
Stomach – Me3deh معدة
Intestines – Msarine مصارين
Brain - Dmegh دماغ
Heart – 2aleb قلب
Kidneys - Klewi كلوي
Lungs - Raweya راوية
Liver – Kebed كبد
Nail – Dofor ضفر
Skeleton – Haykal 3azmi هيكل عظمي
Bone – 3admeh عضمة
Bone – (p) 3dam عضم
Spine – Senslit Daher سنسلة ضهر
Ribs – Dla3 ضلع
Skull – Jemejmeh جمجمة
Skin – Bachara بشرة
Skin – Jeld جلد
Vein – Wareed وريد

He has a problem with his stomach.
3ando mechekleh bi me3edto.
عندو مشكلة بمعدته.

The brain, heart, kidneys, lungs, and liver are internal organs.
El dmegh, el 2aleb, el klewi, el raweya wel kebed kellon a3da2-dekhliyeh (internal organs).
الدماغ، القلب، الكلاوي، الرواية والكبد كلن أعضاء داخلية.

I want to cut my nails.
Baddi 2oss dwafiri.
بدي اقص ضوافري.

I have a cast on my foot because of a broken bone.
3andi jabra 3a 2ejri la2enno 3andi 3admeh maksoura.
عندي جبرا عإجري لأنه عندي عضمة مكسورة.

The spine is the main part of the body.
Senslit el daher hiyeh aham jeze2 (part) bel jesem.
سنسلة الضهر هيي أهم جهاز بالجسم.

I have beautiful skin.
3andi bachera 7elweh.
عندي بشرة حلوة.

Health and medical – So77a w tababeh صحة وطبابة

Disease – Marad مرض
Bacteria – Bacteria بكتيريا
Sick – Marid مريض
Clinic – 3iyedeh عيادة
Headache – Waja3 Ras وجع راس
Earache – Waja3 Dinein وجع دنين
Pharmacy - Saydaliyeh صيدلية
Prescription – Wasfeh وصفة
Symptoms – 3awarid عوارض
Nausea – La3ayen لعيان
Stomachache – Waja3 Me3deh وجع معدة
Allergy – 7asesiyeh حساسية
Penicillin - Penicillin بنسلين
Antibiotic – Antibiotic انتيبيوتك

These bacteria caused this disease.
Hawdeh el bacteria sabbabou (caused) hayda el marad.
هودي البكتيريا سببو هيدا المرض.

He is very sick.
Houeih ktir marid.
هو كتير مريض.

I have a headache so I must go to the pharmacy to refill my prescription.
3andi waja3 ras fa lezim rou7 3al saydaliyeh la 3abbi (refill) el-wasfeh taba3i.
عندي وجع راس فلازم روح عالصيدلية لعبّي الوصفة تبعي.

The main symptoms of food poisoning are nausea and stomach ache.
El 3awarid el 2aseisiyeh lal tasamom (poison) men el akel henneh el la3ayen w waja3 me3deh.
الأعراض الرئيسية للتسمم من الأكل هني لعيان ووجع معدة.

I have an allergy to penicillin, so I need another antibiotic.
3edni 7aseisiyeh 3al penicillin, fa (so) lezemeni gheir (another) antibiotic.
عندي حساسية من البنسلين فلازمني غير انتيبيوتك.

Sore throat – 2eltiheb Bel 7ale2 إلتهاب بالحلق
Fever – 7arara حرارة
Flu – Grippe جربي
Cough – Sa3leh سعالة
To cough – Tes3ol تسعل
Infection – 2eltiheb إلتهاب
Injury – 2isabeh إصابه
Scar – Nedeb ندب
Ache – Waja3, وجع
Ache – (p) 2awje3 أوجاع
Pain – Waja3 وجع
Intensive care – 3ineyeh Fey2a عناية فائقة
Bandaid – Telzi2 Jere7 تلزيق جرح
Bandage – Damadeh ضمادة

Are you in good health?
So7tak meni7a?
صحتك منيحة؟

What do I need to treat an earache?
Shou lezemeni la 3elij waja3 el dayneh?
شو لازمني لعلاج وجع الدينه.

I need to go to the clinic for my fever and sore throat.
Lezim rou7 3al 3iyedeh kermel (for) 7ararti w 2iltiheb 7al2i.
لازم روح عالعياده كرمال حرارتي وإلتهاب حلقي.

The bandage won't help your infection.
El damadeh ma-ra7 (will not) tse3id el 2eltiheb yalli 3endak.
الضمادة مارح تساعد الإتهاب يلي عندك.

I have a serious injury so I must go to intensive care.
2esabti khotra fa lezim rou7 3al 3ineiyeh el fey2a.
إصابتي خطرة فلازم روح عالعناية الفائقة.

Hospital – Mestachfa مستشفى
Doctor – 7akim حكيم
Nurse - Moumarrid ممرض
Nurse - (f) Moumarrida ممرضة
Family Doctor – 7akim El 3ayleh حكيم عيلة
Pediatrician – 7akim 2atfal حكيم أطفال
Medication – 2edewyeh أدوية
Pills – 7boub حبوب
Heartburn – 7ar2a حرقة
Paramedic – Mous3if مسعف
Paramedic – (f) Mous3ifeh مسعفة
Emergency room – Gherfit El taware2 غرفة طوارئ
Health insurance – Ta2meen So77i تأمين صحي
Patient - Marid مريض
Patient - (f) Marida مريضة

Where is the closest hospital?
Wen 2a2rab mestachfa?
وين أقرب مستشفى؟

Usually we see the nurse before the doctor.
3adatan menshouf el moumarid abel el 7akim.
عادةً منشوف الممرض قبل الحكيم.

The paramedics can take her to the emergency room but she doesn't have health insurance.
El mous3ifin bye2edrou yekhdouwa 3a gherfit el tawari2 bass ma 3anda ta2meen so77i.
المسعفين بقدروا ياخدوها عغرفة الطوارئ بس ما عندا تأمين صحي.

The doctor treated the patient.
El 7akim 3elaj el marid.
الحكيم عالج المريض.

I have to take medicine every day.
Lezim ekhod dawa kel yom.
لازم آخد دوا كل يوم.

Do you have any pills for heartburn?
3andak dawa lal 7ar2a?
عندك دوا للحرقة؟

Surgery – Jira7a جراحة
Surgeon – Jerra7 جراح
Anesthesia – Benej بنج
Local anesthesia – Benej Mawda3i بنج موضعي
General anesthesia – Benej 3am بنج عام
Wheelchair – Kersi Met7arrik كرسي متحرك
A walker – El Walker الواكر
A cane – El 3ekkayzeh العكازة
Stretcher – 7ammeleh حمالة
Dialysis – Ghasil Klewi غسيل كلاوي
Insulin - Insuline إنسولين
Diabetes – Sekkari سكري
Temperature – 7arara حرارة
Thermometer – Mizen 7arara ميزان حرارة
A shot – 2ebreh إبرة
Needle – 2ebreh إبرة
Syringe – Seringue سرنجة

He needs knee surgery today.
Lezmo 3amaliyeh bi rekebto lyom.
.لازمو عملية بركبته اليوم

The surgeon needs to administer general anesthesia in order to operate on the patient.
El jerra7 bado ya3mol benej 3am la yballish yechteghil 3al marid.
.الجراح بده يعمل بنج عام ليبلش يشتغل عالمريض

Does the patient need a wheelchair or a stretcher?
El marid baddo kersi met7arrik aw 7emmeleh?
المريض بده كرسي متحرك أو حمالة؟

Where is the closest dialysis center?
Wen 2a2rab centre la ghasil el klewi?
.وين أقرب سنتر لغسيل الكلاوي

The doctor didn't prescribe insulin for my diabetes.
El 7akim ma wasafli insulin lal sekkari taba3i.
.الحكيم ما وصفلي أنسولين للسكري تبعي

I need a thermometer to take my temperature.
Baddi mizein 7arara la 2ekhod 7ararti.
.بدي ميزان حرارة لآخد حرارتي

Stroke – Jalta جلطه
Blood - Damm دم
Blood pressure – Daght El Damm ضغط الدم
Heart attack – Dab7a 2albiyeh دبحة قلبية
Cancer – Saratan سرطان
Chemotherapy – 3ileij kimawi علاج كيماوي
To help – Tse3id تساعد
Germs - Jarasim جراثيم
Virus – Verus فيروس
Vaccine – Louka7 لقاح
A cure – 3ileij علاج
To cure – Tit3elij تتعالج
Nutrition - Taghziyeh تغذية
Diet - Régime رجيم
Cholesterol – Cholesterol كوليسترول

A stroke is caused by a lack of blood flow to the brain.
Sabab el jalta houeih 2en2ita3 el dam 3an el dmegh.
سبب الجلطة هو انقطاع الدم عن الدماغ.

These are the symptoms of a heart attack.
Hawde 3awarid el dab7a el 2albiyeh.
هودي عوارض الدبحة القلبية.

Chemotherapy is for treating cancer.
El-3ileij el-kimawi houeih la 3ileij al-saratan.
العلاج الكيماوي هو لعلاج السرطان.

Proper nutrition is very important and you must avoid foods that are high in cholesterol.
El taghziyeh el mazbouta ktir mhemmeh w lezim tetjannab (avoid) el akel yalli fiyo ktir cholesterol.
التغذية المزبوطة كتير مهمة ولازم تتجنب الأكل يلي فيو كتير كوليسترول.

I am starting my diet today.
Ra7 ballich regime lyom.
رح بلّش رجيم اليوم.

There is no cure for this virus, only a vaccine.
Ma fi 3ileij la hayda el verus, 2ella el louka7.
ما في علاج لهيدا الفيروس إلا لقاح.

Blind – 2a3ma أعمى
Deaf – 2atrach أطرش
Mute – 2akhras أخرس
Young - Chab شب
Elderly – Khetyar ختيار
Fat – Nasa7a نصاحة
Fat (person) – Nasi7 ناصح
Fat (person) – (f) Nas7a ناصحة
Skinny (person) – D3if ضعيف
Nursing home – Dar El Ri3ayeh دار الرعاية
Disability – 2i3aka إعاقة
Handicap – Mou3ak معاق
Paralysis – Chalal شلل
Depression – 2e7bat إحباط
Anxiety – 2ala2 قلق
Dentist – 7akim Snen حكيم سنان
X-ray – Sourit 2ache33a صورة أشعة
Tooth cavity – Souseh سوسة
Tooth paste – Ma3joun Snein معجون سنان
Tooth brush – Fercheyit Snein فرشاية سنان

The nursing home is open 365 days a year.
Dar el ri3ayeih byefta7 365 nhar bel seneih.
دار الرعاية يفتح 365 نهار بالسنة.

I don't like suffering from depression and anxiety.
Ma b7ebb 3eni men el 2e7bat wel 2ala2.
ما بحب عاني من الإحباط والقلق.

Soap and water kill germs.
El saboun wel may bye2etlou (to kill) el jarasim.
الصابون والمي بقتلوا الجراثيم.

The dentist took X-rays of my teeth to check for cavities.
7akim el snein akhad sourit 2ache33a la sneni la yshouf eza-fi (if there is/are) sous.
حكيم السنان أخد صورة أشعة لسناني إزا في سوس.

In the morning I put tooth paste on my toothrbush
El sobo7 b7ott ma3joun snein 3ala fercheyit el snein taba3i.
الصبح بحط معجون السنان على فرشاية السنان تبعي.

Emergency & Disasters – Kawerith w tawari2 — كوارث وطوارئ

Emergency – Tawari2 طوارئ
Help – Mouse3adeh مساعدة
Fire – Nar نار
Ambulance – Siyarit 2es3af سيارة إسعاف
First aid – 2es3af إسعاف
CPR – Tanaffos 2istina3i تنفس اصطناعي
Accident – 7edis حادث
Car crash – 7edis Siyara حادث سيارة
Death - Mot موت
Deadly – mumeet مميت
Fatality – Da7iyyeh ضحية
Lightly wounded – 2isabeh Khafifeh إصابة خفيفة
Moderately wounded – 2isabeh Wasat إصابة وسط
Seriously wounded – 2isabeh Khotra إصابة خطرة

There is a fire. I need to call for help.
Fi 7ari2. Lezim 2otlob mouse3adeh.
.في حريق، لازم أطلب مساعدة

I need to call an ambulance.
Lezim de2 (to call) la siyarit el-2es3af.
.لازم دق لسيارة الإسعاف

That accident was bad.
Haydek el 7edis ken awi.
.هديك الحادث كان قوي

The car crash was fatal, there were two deaths, and four suffered serious injuries.
7edis el siyara kein mumeet, met tnein, w 2arb3a nsabou 2isabet awiyeh.
.حادث السيارة كان مميت، مات اتنين و أربعة انصابوا إصابات قوية

One was moderately wounded and two were lightly wounded.
Wa7ad nsab 2isabeh wasat w tnen 2isabet khafifeh.
.واحد انصاب إصابه وسط وتنين إصابات خفيفة

CPR is a first step of first-aid.
El tanaffos el 2istina3i awal-khotweh (first line) men el 2is3afet el awwaliyeh (first).
.التنفس الإصطناعي أول خطوة من الإسعافات الأولية

Emergency number – Ra2m el Tawari2 رقم الطوارئ
Fire truck – Siyarit El 2itfa2 سيارة الإطفاء
Siren – Zammour Khatar زامور خطر
Fire extinguisher – Toffayet 7ari2 طفاية حريق
Police - Chorta شرطة
Police station – Makhfar مغفر
Robbery – Ser2a سرقة
Thief – Serra2 سراق / **Thief** – 7arami حرامي
Fire hydrant – Sanbour El 2itfa2 صنبور الإطفاء
Fireman – 2etfa2i إطفائي
Emergency situation – 7alit Tawari2 حالة طوارئ

The police are on their way.
El chorta jeyeh (on the way).
الشرطة جاية.

I must call the police station to report a robbery.
Lezim de2 lal makhfar (police station) la balligh (to report) 3an el ser2a.
لازم دق للمخفر لبلّغ عن السارق.

The siren of the fire truck is very loud.
Zammour el khatar taba3 (of the) siyarit el 2itfa2 ktir 3ali (loud/high).
زامور الخطر تبع سيارة الإطفاء عالي.

Where is the fire extinguisher?
Wen tofayet el 7ari2?
وين طفاية الحريق؟

Please provide me with the emergency number.
3mol ma3rouf a3tini ra2em el tawari2.
اعمل معروف اعطيني رقم الطوارئ.

It's prohibited to park by the fire hydrant in case of a fire.
Mamenou3 (prohibited) tsoff 7add sanbour el 7ari2 2eza fi 7ari2.
ممنوع تصف حد صنبور الحريق إزا في حريق.

When there is a fire, the first to arrive on scene are the firemen.
Wa2et ykoun fi 7ari2 awal elli byousalou henneh el 2etfa2iyeh.
وقت يكون في حريق أول الي بوصلوا هني الإطفائية.

There is a fire. I must call for help.
Fi 7ari2. Lezim otlob mouse3adeh.
في حريق، لازم أطلب المساعدة.

In an emergency situation everyone needs to be rescued.
Bi 7alit al-tawari2 el kell lezim yetkhallasou (rescue).
بحالة الطوارئ الكل لازم يتخلّصوا.

Natural disaster – Kerseh Tabi3iyeh كارثة طبيعية
Destruction – Damar دمار
Damage – Darar ضرر
Hurricane – 2e3sar إعصار
Refuge – Malja2 ملجئ
Caused – Sabbab سبّب
Tornado – 2e3sar اعصار
Flood – Fayadan فيضان
Storm – 3asfeh عاصفة
Snowstorm – 3asfit Talej عاصفة تلج
Hail – Barad برَد
Safety – 2amein أمان
Drought – Jafef جفاف
Famine – Maje3a مجاعة
Poverty – Fo2or فقر
Epidemic – Wabe2 وباء
Pandemic – Je2i7a جائحة
Explosion – 2infijar انفجار
Rescue – 2inkaz انقاذ

The tornado destroyed the town.
El 2e3sar kassar el mdineh.
الإعصار كسّر المدينة.

The drought led to famine and a lot of poverty.
El jafef sabbab la maje3a w fo2or ktir.
الجفاف سبب مجاعة وفقر كتير.

There were three days of flooding following the storm.
Ken-fi (there were) fayadanet la tlet 2iymeh men-ba3d el 3asfeh.
كان في فياضانات لتلات أيام من بعد العاصفة.

This is a snowstorm and not a hail storm.
Hayde 3asfit talej mech 3asfit barad.
هيدي عاصفة تلج مش عاصفة برَد.

The gas explosion led to a natural disaster.
2infijar el ghaz sabbab bi kerseh tabi3iyeh.
انفجار الغاز سبب بكارثة طبيعية.

The hurricane caused a lot of damage and destruction in its path.
El 2e3sar sabbab ktir darar w damar bi tari2o.
الإعصار سبب كتير ضرر ودمار بطريقه.

Dangerous – Khotir خطير
Danger – Khatar خطر
Warning – Te7zir تحذير
Earthquake – Hazzeh 2ardiyeh هزة أرضية
Disaster – Kerseh كارثة
Disaster area – Manta2a Mankoubeh منطقة منكوبة
Evacuation – 2ekhle2 إخلاء
Mandatory – 2ejbari إجباري
Safe place – Ma7al 2emin محل آمن
Blackout – 2at3it Kahraba قطعت كهربا
Rainstorm – 3asifit Cheteh عاصفة شتا
Lightning – Bare2 برق
Thunder – Ra3d رعد
Avalanche – 2inhiyar Talji انهيار تلجي
Heatwave – Mawjit Chob موجة شوب
Rip current – Tayyar تيار
Tsunami – Tsunami تسونامي
Whirlpool – Zawba3a زوبعة

We need to evacuate the buildings during the earthquake.
Lezim nekhli el bineyeh bi wa2et el hazzeh.
لازم نخلي البناية بوقت الهزة.

This is a disaster area, therefore there is a mandatory evacuation order.
Haydeh manta2a (area) mankoubeh, menhek (therefore) fi 2amer 2ekhle2 2ejbari.
هيدي منطقة منكوبة ، من هيك في أمر إخلاء إجباري.

Due to the rainstorm there was a blackout for three hours.
Men wara el cheteh n2ata3it el kahraba tlet se3at.
من ورا الشتا انقطعت الكهربا تلات ساعات.

Be careful during the snowstorm, because there might be an avalanche.
Ntebih (be careful) bi 3asfit el talej, la2enno ma32oul (possible) ysir 2inhiyar talji.
انتبه بعاصفة التلج ، لأنه معقول يصير انهيار تلجي.

There is a risk of lightning today.
Fi khatar ra3d lyom.
في خطر رعد اليوم.

House – El bet البيت

Living room – 2oudit el 2a3deh أوضة القعدة
Room – 2ouda أوضة
Couch – Kanabeyeh كناباي
Sofa – Sofa صوفا
Door – Beb باب
Closet – Khzeneh خزانة
Stairway – Daraj درج
Curtain – Berdeyeh برداي
Window – Chebbek شباك
Floor – 2ared أرض
Floor (as in level) – Tabi2 طابق

The living room is missing a couch.
2oudit el 2a3deh na2isa kanabeyeh.
أوضة القعدة ناقصا كناباي

The attic is an extra room in the house.
El 3elliyeh hyeh matra7 zyedeh (extra/additional) bel bet.
العليّه هي مطرح زيادة بالبيت.

I must buy a new door for my closet.
Lezim echtri beb jdid lal khzeneh.
لازم أشتري باب جديد للخزانة.

The spiral staircase is beautiful.
El daraj el mabroum 7elou.
الدرج المبروم حلو.

There aren't any curtains on the windows.
Ma fi wala baradi 3al chebbik.
ما في ولا برادي عالشباك.

I have a marble floor on the first floor and a wooden floor on the second floor.
3andi 2aredieh rkhem bel tabi2 el 2awal, w 2aredieh khachab (wooden) bel tabi2 el teni.
عندي أرضية رخام بالطابق الأول، وأرضية خشب بالطابق التاني.

Rug – Sejjedeh سجادة
Balcony – Balcon بلكون
Carpet – Sejjedeh سجاده
Doormat – Mamsa7a ممسحة
Attic – 3elliyeh علّيه
Basement – 2abou قبو
Fireplace – Maw2adeh موقده
Chimney – Madkhaneh مدخنة
Trash – Zbeleh زبالة
Garbage can – Sallit El Zbeleh سلة زبالة
Driveway – Tari2 Khas طريق خاص
Jar – Mortben مرتبان

I can clean the floors today and then I want to arrange the closet.
Fyi naddif (to clean) el 2ared lyom w ba3den badi zabbit (to arrange) el khzeneh.
فيي نضّف الأرض اليوم وبعدين بدي زبط الخزانة.

I have to wash the rug with laundry detergent.
Lezim ghassil el sejjedeh bi dawa ghasil.
لازم غسّل السجادة بدوا الغسيل.

I can install new windows for my balcony.
Fyi rakkib (to install) chbebik jded lal balcon 3endi (my).
فيي ركّب شباك جديد للبلكونة عندي.

I must install a new roof.
Lezim rakkib sate7 jdid.
لازم ركّب سطح جديد.

The fire sparkles in the fireplace.
El nar 3am betchar2it (sparkles) bel maw2adeh.
النار عم بتشرئط بالموقدة.

All the glass jars are outside on the doormat.
Kell mratbin el 2zez barra 3al mamsa7a.
كل مراتبين القزاز برا عالممسحة.

The garbage can is blocking the driveway.
Sallit el zbeleh msakkra el tari2.
سلة الزبالة مسكرة الطريق

Silverware – Foddiyet فضيات
Knife - Sekkin سكين
Fork - Chawkeh شوكة
Spoon – Mel3a2a ملعقة
Teaspoon – Mel3a2it Chay ملعقة شاي
Kitchen – Matbakh مطبخ
A cup – Kebbeyeh كوباي
Plate – Sa7en صحن
Bowl – Keseh كيسة
Napkin – Ma7rameh محرمة
Table – Tawleh طاولة
Placemat – Mafrach Sofra مفرش سفرة
Roof – Sate7 سطح
Ceiling – Sa2ef سقف
Wall – 7et حيط

The color of my ceiling is white.
Lon el sa2ef 3andi 2abyad.
لون السقف عندي أبيض.

I must paint the walls.
Lezim 2edhan el 7itan.
لازم أدهن الحيطان.

The knives, spoons, teaspoons, and forks are inside the drawer in the kitchen.
El skekin, el male3i2, male3i2 el chay wel chouwak kellon bi 2aleb el jarour bel matbakh.
السكين، الملعقة، ملعقة الشاي والشوك كلون بقلب الجارور بالمطبخ.

There aren't enough cups, plates, and silverware on the table for everyone.
Ma fi kebbeyet, s7oun, w foddiyet kefyin lal kell 3al tawleh.
ما في كوبايات، صحون وفضيات كافيين للكل عالطاولة.

The napkin is underneath the bowl.
El ma7rameh ta7et (underneath) el keseh.
المحرمة تحت الكيسة.

The placemats are on the table.
El maferich 3al tawleh.
المفارش عالطاولة.

Table cloth – Ghata Al Tawleh غطا الطاولة
Glass (material) – 2zez قزاز
A glass (cup) – Kebbeyet 2zez كباية قزاز
Oven - Foron فرن / **Stove** – Ghaz غاز
Pot (cooking) – Casserole كاسيرول
Pan – Me2leyeh مقلاية
Shelve – Raff رف
Cabinet – Khzenet Matbakh خزانة مطبخ
Pantry – Makhzan مخزن
Drawer – Jarour جارور

The table cloth is beautiful.
Ghata el tawleh 7elou.
غطا الطاولة حلو.

There is canned food in the pantry.
Fi m3allabet bel makhzan.
في معلبات بالمخزن.

Where are the toothpicks?
Wen el curdents?
وين الكرتينز؟

The glasses on the shelve are used for champagne, not wine.
El kebbeyet elli 3al raff lal champagne, mech lal mbid.
الكبايات اللي عالرف للشانبين مش للنبيد.

The pizza is in the oven.
El pizza bel foron.
البيتزا بالفرن.

The pots and pans are in the cabinet.
El casserole wel me2leyet bel khzeneh.
الكسترول والمقلايات بالخزانة.

The stove isn't functioning.
El ghaz ma 3am yemchi.
الغاز ما عم يمشي.

Bedroom – 2ouditl El Nom أوضة نوم
Bed - Takhet تخت
Blanket – Bottaniyeh بطانية
Bed sheet – Charchaf El Takhet شرشف التخت
Mattress - Farcheh فرشة
Pillow – Mkhaddeh مخده
Mirror – Mreyeh مراية
Chair – Kersi كرسي
Dinning room – 2oudit El Sofra أوضة سفرة
Hallway – El Entrée الإنتري
Downstairs – El-Tabi2 elli Ta7et الطابق اللي تحت
Garden – Jnayneh جنينة
Backyard – Jnayneh جنينة

The master bedroom is at the end of the hallway, and the dining room is downstairs.
El 2ouda el kbireh bi ekhir el entrée, w 2oudit el sofra bel tabi3 elli ta7et.
الأوضة الكبيرة بآخر الإنتري وأوضة السفرة بالطابق اللي تحت.

The mirror looks good in the bedroom.
El mreyeh mbayneh meni7a bel 7emmem.
المراي مبينة منيحة بالحمام.

I have to buy a new bed and a new mattress.
Lezim 2echtri takhet jdid w farcheh jdideh.
لازم أشتري تخت جديد و فرشة جديدة.

Where are the blankets and bed sheets?
Wen el bottaniyet w charachif el takhet?
وين البطانيات وشرشف التخت؟

My pillows are on the chair.
Mkhaddeti 3al kersi.
مخدتي عالكرسي.

The kids are playing either in the basement or the backyard.
El wled 3am yel3abou aw bel 2abou 2aw bel jnayneh.
الولاد عم يلعبوا أو بالقبو أو بالجنينة.

Towel – Manchafeh منشفة
Bathtub - Bagno بقنو
Shower - Douche دش
Soap – Saboun صابون
Bathroom – 7emmem حمام
Sink – Maghsaleh مغسلة
Bag - Kis كيس
Box – Sandoo2 صندوق
Keys – Mfeti7 مفتاح
Candle – Cham3a شمعة
Laundry - Ghasil غسيل

These towels are for drying your hand.
Hawdeh el manechif henneh la tenchif (to dry) el 2iden.
هودي المناشف هني لتنشيف الإيدين.
The bathtub, shower, and the sink are old.
El bagno, el douche, wel maghsaleh kellon (they are all) 2dem (old).
البقنو، الدش والمغسلة كلن قدام.
I need soap to wash my hands.
Baddi saboun la ghassil (to wash) 2idayyi.
بدي صابون لغسّل إيدي.
The guest bathroom is in the corner of the hallway.
7emmem el dyouf bi zewyit (corner) el entrée.
حميام الضيوف بزاوية الإنتري.
How many boxes does he have?
Kam sandoo2 3endo?
كم صندوق عنده؟
I can only light this candle now.
Ma be2dir gher dawwi hal cham3a halla2.
ما بقدر غير ضوي هالشمعة هلأ.
I want to put my items in the plastic bag.
Badi 7ott ghradi (items) bi kis el plastic.
بدي حط غراضي بكيس البلاستك.
I need to bring my keys.
Lezim jib mfeti7i.
لازم جيب مفتاحي.

If you enjoyed this book but missed "Part-1" and "Part-3" then feel free to check them out on Amazon.

Conclusion

You have now learned a wide range of sentences in relation to a variety of topics such as the home and garden. You can discuss the roof and ceiling of a house, plus natural disasters like hurricanes and thunderstorms.

The combination of sentences can also work well when caught in a natural disaster and having to deal with emergency issues. When the electricity gets cut you can tell your family or friends, "I can only light this candle now." As you're running out of the house, remind yourself of the essentials by saying, "I need to bring my keys with me."

If you need to go to a hospital, you have now been provided with sentences and the vocabulary for talking to doctors and nurses and dealing with surgery and health issues. Most importantly, you can ask, "What is the emergency number in this country?" When you get to the hospital, tell the health services, "The hurricane caused a lot of destruction and damage in its path," and "We used the hurricane shelter for refuge."

The three hundred and fifty words that you learned in part 1 should have been a big help to you with these new themes. When learning the Lebanese dialect of the Arabic language, you are now more able to engage with people in Lebanon, which should make your travels flow a lot easier.

Part 3 will introduce you to additional topics that will be invaluable to your journeys. You will learn vocabulary in relation to politics, the military, and the family. The three books in this series all together provide a flawless system of learning Lebanese Arabic. When you visit Spain or Latin America you will now have the capacity for greater conversational learning.

When you proceed to Part 3 you will be able to expand your vocabulary and conversational skills even further. Your range of topics will expand to the office environment, business negotiations and even school.

Please, feel free to post a review in order to share your experience or suggest feedback as to how this method can be improved.

NOTE FROM THE AUTHOR

Thank you for your interest in my work. I encourage you to share your overall experience of this book by posting a review. Your review can make a difference! Please feel free to describe how you benefited from my method or provide creative feedback on how I can improve this program. I am constantly seeking ways to enhance the quality of this product, based on personal testimonials and suggestions from individuals like you.

Thanks and best of luck,

Yatir Nitzany

Also by Yatir Nitzany

Conversational Spanish Quick and Easy

Conversational French Quick and Easy

Conversational Italian Quick and Easy

Conversational Portuguese Quick and Easy

Conversational German Quick and Easy

Conversational Dutch Quick and Easy

Conversational Norwegian Quick and Easy

Conversational Danish Quick and Easy

Conversational Russian Quick and Easy

Conversational Ukrainian Quick and Easy

Conversational Bulgarian Quick and Easy

Conversational Polish Quick and Easy

Conversational Hebrew Quick and Easy

Conversational Yiddish Quick and Easy

Conversational Armenian Quick and Easy

Conversational Romanian Quick and Easy

Conversational Arabic Quick and Easy
Modern Standard Arabic

Conversational Arabic Quick and Easy
Palestinian Dialect

....

Conversational Arabic Quick and Easy
Syrian Dialect

....

Conversational Arabic Quick and Easy
Jordanian Dialect

....

Conversational Arabic Quick and Easy
Egyptian Dialect

....

Conversational Arabic Quick and Easy
Moroccan Dialect

....

Conversational Arabic Quick and Easy
Tunisian Dialect

....

Conversational Arabic Quick and Easy
Saudi (Hejazi, Najdi & Gulf) Dialect

....

Conversational Arabic Quick and Easy
Iraqi Dialect

....

Conversational Arabic Quick and Easy
Emirati Dialect

....

Conversational Arabic Quick and Easy
Qatari Dialect

....

Conversational Arabic Quick and Easy
Kuwaiti Dialect